"Hello, World!"
A History of Programming

PROFESSOR JAMES STEINBERG

CONTENTS

1 INTRODUCTION

Computers are a part of everyday life – wherever you look, there is likely to be a computer behind the scenes. Hand-in-hand with the physical computer (the chips and other hardware), is the software that runs on it. When most people think of software, they will usually only think of programs such as word processors or spreadsheets or even the latest "third person shoot-'em up" that they play on their X-Box. Software goes much further than that though – consider your washing machine. When you turn the dial (or press the button) to start the 40° wash, you are actually interacting with a program which will control the machine during that wash.

So, how did that program that you are using get produced? The answer is by programmers using a programming language. There are thousands of programming languages in existence – some are extremely popular and used for many things, others are specialist or have been assigned to history.

This book seeks to explore the history of programming, from its early beginnings before the invention of computers (yes that is right – programming came before computers), through to the modern programming languages that are used today.

The history of programming languages can be described in one of two ways. Firstly, there is the generational language classification system, that classifies languages as getting more abstract. Secondly, the developments can be described in terms of the chronological history of their development. It is important to understand that the "generations" overlap, for example with third generation languages continuing to be developed and designed after the initial introduction of fourth generation languages.

In Chapter 2, we take a brief look at the pre-history of computers in the 19th century. Chapter 3 gives an overview of the generations classification and then the subsequent chapters explore in depth the important developments since the beginning of the modern computer age and my thoughts for the future of programming.

Chapter 10 describes the process of writing a program in the early 1970s and is based on the recollections of a programmer working for IBM at the time.

Some of the original high level languages from the 1950s are still in use today, over half a century later. These languages have evolved over time, taking in ideas from more recent languages and paradigms. In chapter 11, we look at the evolution of the FORTRAN language, by comparing the coding of the same program in the various versions.

Chapter 12 provides a humorous alternative look at the history of programming that I came across while surfing the web.

Chapter 13 takes a look at another feature of programming languages that has changed over time during the history of programming, that of programming paradigms.

Chapter 14 takes a look at the area of esoteric programming languages and why they are created.

In chapter 15, we look at something that had gone hand in hand with programming throughout its history – the 'bug'.

Finally, in chapter 16, there is a comparison of a number of languages using the popular "Hello, World!" program (hence the name of the book). This program is often the first that a newcomer will write in a language and does nothing more than output the phrase "Hello, World!".

2 LOOMS AND LOVELACE

The first programming languages predate the modern computer by well over a century. These first languages have no comparison to the complex languages that exist today and were in fact just codes.

In 1801, Joseph Marie Jacquard invented the Jacquard Loom, a mechanical loom controlled by punched cards.

Although the Jacquard Loom did no computation on the punched card inputs, it is considered an important step in the history of computers. An important feature of the loom was that the pattern of its weave could be changed by simply changing the cards and this was an important concept in the development of computer programming.

Jump forward nearly four decades to 1837 and Charles Babbage, who was known as the Father of Computing, first described his Analytical Engine, which was a successor to his Difference Engine. The Analytical Engine was designed to be a general purpose computer, which could be programmed by means of punched cards.

In 1843, Ada Byron, Countess of Lovelace translated a description of the Analytical Engine written by Luigi Menabrea into English. As part of the translation, Ada added additional notes. One of these notes was an algorithm for the Analytical Engine to compute Bernoulli numbers. This algorithm was considered the first to be specifically written for implementation on a computer and Ada is often cited as being the first computer programmer.

This pre-history of computing is however, entirely conceptual as neither the Difference Engine or the Analytical Engine were built in Babbage or Ada's lifetimes. It was not until a century later that the first general purpose computers were actually built and it is there that the real history of programming languages begins.

In the mid 1930s, a need to understand more about the nature of computation led to two early programming formalisms – Turing machines and Lambda calculus.

Alan Turing wrote a paper introducing an abstract machine with which to study the nature of computing. A Turing machine is a 7-tuple – M = <Q, T, I, δ , b, q_0, q_f>, where –

- Q is a finite, non-empty set of states,
- T is a finite, non-empty set of the tape alphabet/symbols,
- I is the set of input symbols, I $\subseteq$ T,
- δ is the transition function,
- b $\in$ T \ I is the designated symbol for a blank,
- q_0 is the initial state, and
- q_f is the final or accepting state.

The transition function δ governs the operation of the Turing machine.

At each step in its operation, the Turing machine examines an input symbol on the tape, writes a symbol and moves the tape according to its current state and the transition function δ. This process will continue until the final state is reached.

Lambda calculus (λ-calculus) is a formal system for expressing computation using value binding and substitution. Lambda calculus was first formulated by Alonzo Church at the Princeton Institute of Advanced Studies. Lambda calculus expressions form the underlying basis of the functional programming paradigm.

Every lambda expression is a function or an application of a function to an argument and every algorithm can be expressed as a lambda expression. Unlike the Turing machines, Lambda calculus does not exhibit any time-variant behavior.

3 GENERATIONAL CLASSIFICATION

Modern computer programming language development can be thought of as going through five overlapping generations, although the concept of these generations was not really introduced until the third generation.

The first generation actually consisted of only one language, machine language. This was the direct entry of binary code (0's and 1's) into the computer. In the early days of computers, this was often achieved by directly manipulating switches and dials on the front of the computer to represent the code being entered. These early computers also had no permanent storage, so programs had to be re-entered each time they were required.

Similarly, the second generation is deemed to be just one language, assembly language. Assembly language was a low level language where each instruction represented one machine code operation. Assembly language had mnemonics to represent the operation part of the code, which made it easier for humans to understand.

Although both machine language and assembly language are each deemed to be one language, there were in fact many different flavours of each. Each different computer architecture would have its own version of the languages with different instructions.

The third generation languages began to evolve in the 1950s and continue to be in use today. These were general purpose languages, such as FORTRAN, COBOL, C and Pascal. These languages differ widely in terms of their syntax, but they all share enhancements in logical structure over assembly language. There is also a greater level of abstraction from machine code, with a single line of third generation language code representing a number of lines of assembly or machine code.

The introduction of fourth generation languages in the 1970s looked to move away from the general purpose languages and into application specific languages. This included languages such as SQL, SAS and ColdFusion.

In the 1980s, the fifth generation of programming languages was defined. These languages tend to be more researched based than operational and are not commercially available. One defining feature of these languages is that they are constraint based rather than algorithmically designed. The idea was that it would not be necessary for a programmer to worry about how to solve a problem, just what the problem is and what the constraints were.

3 THE 1940S

In the early 1940s, the first modern computers were created. These enormous machines did not have the keyboards and mice that we are used to today. Input was done using punched cards or using individual switches on the front of the computer. However, on the inside, logically the computers worked in much the same way as they do today, using binary logic (the representation of 0's and 1's) to store data and programs.

The programming of these early computers was done using machine code – directly inputting the 0's and 1's that represented a particular instruction. Each instruction performs a very specific task, such as an add operation on a unit of data and an executable program is made up of a series of many thousands of these atomic instructions.

Each instruction is made up of a set number of bits, which are sub-divided to hold details of the operation to be performed and what numbers it is to be performed on. For example, in a 32 bit long instruction, the instruction to add the contents of registers 1 and 2 and store the result in register 6 could be written as:

000000 00001 00010 00110 00000 100000

Whilst machine language speaks in the language of the machine (hence the name), it is not easily readable by humans. Imagine that the example above is just one line in a program that could consist of many thousands of lines of similar instructions and you can see why. In fact in "CONTU Revisited: The Case against Copyright Protection for Computer Programs in Machine-Readable Form", Pamela Stevenson indicates that machine code is so unreadable that the United States Copyright Office cannot even identify whether a particular encoded program is an original work of authorship.

Although introduced in the early years of computers, machine code still operates at the heart of all computers. Programs written today in the higher level languages are still internally translated into machine code to enable them to be run on the computer.

In the late 1940s, the second generation of programming languages was introduced. This was assembly language, which is a low-level programming language where each statement corresponds to an individual machine code instruction. The assembly language program is converted into executable machine code by a program referred to as an assembler. As with machine code, assembly languages were specific to a particular type of computer.

Assembly language uses a mnemonic to represent each machine code operation, followed by one or more operands to represent the data to be operated on. Assembly language is a step away from machine code and is more humanly readable, allowing for easier programming and debugging.

As an example, consider the code required to move the value 97 into the AL register. The assembly language to do this could be:

```
MOV AL, 61h
```

This line of code can be broken down as follows:

- First comes the mnemonic MOV, which tells the processor that it is moving a value to a register.
- Then comes the register that the value is to be moved into – in this case the AL register.
- Finally, we specify the value that is to be moved. This is specified in hexadecimal as 61.

One of the benefits of assembly language code is that it is easier for a human to read and therefore be able to understand what the program is doing and how it is doing it. This in turn makes it easier to find and fix any errors that occur in the program.

Whilst many of today's high-level languages can produce code that when compiled can run as fast as hand-written assembly, there are still niche areas where assembly language is important.

For example, assembly is often used where a compact stand-alone executable is required that does not need the libraries and run-time components that are often associated with high level languages. This is often seen in code that is required to run things such as household appliances and other electrical equipment. Another use of assembly is where direct interaction with the computer hardware is required, such as in the implementation of device drivers.

Such is the continued importance of assembly language, that it is still taught in many computer science programs. It is also deemed to be an important method in gaining a grasp of how the computer operates at hardware level and for introducing concepts such as memory allocation.

Further developments in computing saw the introduction of the third generation of programming languages, or higher-level languages as they were known. These languages are closer to human language than they are to the actual machine language that the computers run. These languages were designed to be easier to use for programmers and thus reduce the number of bugs and increase code reuse.

In 1945, John von Neumann began the development of two important concepts that would have a direct impact on future computer programming languages. His first concept, which was known as "shared-program technique" stated that computer hardware should be simple and not need to be hand-wired for each program. Instead, complex instructions should be used to control this simple hardware, allowing for much faster reprogramming. His second concept, referred to as "conditional control transfer". Gave rise to the notation of subroutines and conditional logic such as IF THEN statements and looping using FOR statements. This concept changed programs from a single set of chronologically executed steps to the structured programs that we see today.

In 1948, Konrad Zuse published a paper about his programming language Plankalkül (Plan Calculus). Plankalkül was designed for engineering purposes between 1943 and 1945. It is deemed to be the first high-level programming language to be designed, but was not implemented until 1998 and Zuse's contributions were isolated from other developments that started to take place in the decade that followed.

Important languages of the 1940s

Year	Language	Predecessor(s)
1943–45	Plankalkül (concept)	
1943–46	ENIAC coding system	
1946	ENIAC Short Code	ENIAC coding system
1947	ARC Assembly	ENIAC coding system
1948	CPC Coding Scheme	Babbage's Analytical Engine order code
1948	Curry Notation System	ENIAC coding system
1948	Plankalkül (concept published)	
1949	Brief Code	ENIAC Short Code
1949	C-10	ENIAC Short Code
1949	Seeber coding system	CPC Coding Scheme

5 THE 1950S AND 1960S

It was during the late 1950s and 1960s, that the development and introduction of the first modern programming languages took place and descendents of these languages are still in widespread use today.

1957 saw the introduction of the first implemented high-level language, FORTRAN (FORmula TRANslator). FORTRAN was designed by IBM for use in scientific and engineering computing. FORTRAN's origins can be traced to John W. Backus, who in 1953 submitted a proposal to his superiors at IBM for the development of a practical alternative to assembly language. A draft specification for the language was completed by the middle of 1954, with the first compiler being delivered in April 1957.

The initial version of FORTRAN supported 32 statements and introduced concepts such as IF, DO and GOTO and the use of data-types such as integers and doubles.

FORTRAN has now been in use for over 50 years and has undergone a number of innovations during that time, but has remained backwards compatible to the original language. These innovations have been driven by the trends and paradigms that were in vogue at the time of their release. For example, the Fortran 2003 release added object-oriented support and Fortran 2008 introduced support for concurrent programming.

In 1958, John McCarthy of MIT created the LISt Processing (LISP) language for use in artificial intelligence research. LISP differs from other languages in that its only data-type is the list, which are denoted as a sequence of items enclosed by parentheses. Due to its specialised nature, LISP remains in use to this day and has features that are tough to equal in any modern language.

An additional innovation that came with LISP was the way the language was described. The language syntax was described using a mathematically exact notation called Backus-Naur Form (BNF). Nearly all subsequent programming languages have used a variation of BNF to describe their syntax.

Like FORTRAN, LISP has evolved a great deal since its earliest versions and there have been a number of dialects during that time. The most common current dialects are Scheme and Common Lisp.

Also in 1958, ALGOL (ALGOrithmic Language) a language for scientific use was created by a committee of European and American computer scientists. ALGOL implemented some novel concepts, such as the recursive calling of functions and served as a root of the family tree that eventually produced languages such as Pascal, C and Java.

Whilst ALGOL has influenced a number of current languages, there has been no development of the language itself over the last 30 years. The last major version of ALGOL was S-algol, which was released in 1979.

Initially limited to the scientific fraternity, computing began to take off in the business environment in the late 1950s. Whilst FORTRAN, LISP and ALGOL were very good at handling complex numerical calculations, they were not so good at handling input and output (ALGOL 58 did not have any input/output facilities), which were important in business computing.

In the mid to late 1950s, work done by Grace Hopper and her team at the Remington Rand Corporation identified that business users were uncomfortable with the mathematical notation used in programming languages. They proposed the data-processing problems should be expressed using English keywords. Their work led to the development of FLOW-MATIC, which was previously called B-0 (Business Language version 0).

COBOL (COmmon Business Oriented Language) was developed in 1959 to address this issue. The specifications of the language drew a great inspiration from the Grace Hopper's work on the FLOW-MATIC language and she is often referred to as the "mother of COBOL". COBOL statements have a very English-like grammar, which makes it easy to learn, particularly for businessmen. An example of a COBOL statement is:

ADD YEARS TO AGE

In 1964, the Beginners All-purpose Symbolic Instruction Code (BASIC) was designed by John Kennedy and Thomas Kurtz at Dartmouth College. BASIC was designed to be an easy first language for programming newcomers. Original BASIC had a syntax that included a line number for each line and program control consisted of GOTO # and GOSUB # statements that transferred control to the given line number.

BASIC has enjoyed popularity since its introduction, particularly during the early years of personal computers, where it was often a standard feature. Its presence allowed small business and home users to develop their own custom applications and opened up the availability of computers to businesses that would not previously been able to afford them.

Even today, nearly 50 years after its introduction, BASIC can still be seen in use in areas such as scripting languages for application suites such as Microsoft Office and Open Office. It has developed a long way from the early version and no longer has line numbers and now features object-oriented concepts, but the basic structure and syntax can still be seen.

Whilst it is no longer in common use, the Basic Combined Programming Language (BCPL), which was designed in 1966, has played an important part in programming language development, as we will see below.

BCPL led to a stripped down version, which was called B. B first appeared in the late 1960s and had many of the features of BCPL that B's designers deemed unnecessary removed to make it fit into the memory capacity of the microcomputers that were available at the time. It was this language on which the popular C language was based.

Important languages of the 1950s and 1960s

Year	Language	Predecessor(s)
1950	Short Code	Brief Code
1950	Birkbeck Assembler	ARC
1951	Superplan	Plankalkül
1951	ALGAE	
1951	Intermediate Programming Language	Short Code
1951	Regional Assembly Language	EDSAC
1951	Boehm unnamed coding system	CPC Coding scheme
1951	Klammerausdrücke	Plankalkül
1951	OMNIBAC Symbolic Assembler	Short Code
1951	Stanislaus (Notation)	
1951	Whirlwind assembler	EDSAC
1951	Rochester assembler	EDSAC
1951	Sort Merge Generator	
1952	A-0	C-10 and Short Code
1952	Autocode	CPC Coding scheme
1952	Editing Generator	SORT/MERGE
1952	COMPOOL	
1953	Speedcoding	
1953	READ/PRINT	
1954	Laning and Zierler system	
1954	Mark I Autocode	Glennie Autocode
1954–55	Fortran (concept)	Speedcoding
1954	ARITH-MATIC	A-0
1954	MATH-MATIC	A-0
1954	MATRIX MATH	
1954	IPL I (concept)	
1955	FLOW-MATIC	A-0
1955	BACAIC	
1955	PACT I	FORTRAN, A-2
1955–56	Sequentielle Formelübersetzung	Boehm

Year	Language	Predecessor(s)
1955–56	IT	Laning and Zierler
1955	PRINT	
1956–58	LISP (concept)	IPL
1957	COMTRAN	FLOW-MATIC
1957	Fortran I (implementation)	FORTRAN
1957–58	UNICODE	MATH-MATIC
1957	COMIT (concept)	
1958	IPL II (implementation)	IPL I
1958	Fortran II	FORTRAN I
1958	ALGOL 58 (IAL)	FORTRAN, IT and Sequentielle Formelübersetzung
1958	IPL V	IPL II
1959	FACT	
1959	COBOL (concept)	FLOW-MATIC, COMTRAN, FACT
1959	JOVIAL	ALGOL 58
1959	LISP (implementation)	IPL
1959	MAD – Michigan Algorithm Decoder	ALGOL 58
1959	TRAC (concept)	
1960	ALGOL 60	ALGOL 58
1960	COBOL 61 (implementation)	FLOW-MATIC, COMTRAN
1961	COMIT (implementation)	
1962	Fortran IV	FORTRAN II
1962	APL (concept)	
1962	Simula (concept)	ALGOL 60
1962	SNOBOL	FORTRAN II, COMIT
1963	CPL	ALGOL 60
1963	SNOBOL3	SNOBOL
1963	ALGOL 68 (concept)	ALGOL 60
1963	JOSS I	ALGOL 58
1964	MIMIC	MIDAS
1964	COWSEL	CPL, LISP

Year	Language	Predecessor(s)
1964	PL/I (concept)	ALGOL 60, COBOL, FORTRAN
1964	BASIC	FORTRAN II, JOSS
1964	IBM RPG	FARGO
1964	Mark-IV	
1964	Speakeasy-2	Speakeasy
1964	TRAC (implementation)	
1964?	IITRAN	
1965	MAD/I (concept)	MAD, ALGOL 60, PL/I
1965	TELCOMP	JOSS
1965	Atlas Autocode	Algol 60, Autocode
1966	JOSS II	JOSS I
1966	ALGOL W	ALGOL 60
1966	Fortran 66	FORTRAN IV
1966	ISWIM (Concept)	LISP
1966	CORAL66	ALGOL 60
1967	BCPL	CPL
1967	MUMPS	FORTRAN, TELCOMP
1967	APL (implementation)	
1967	Simula 67 (implementation)	ALGOL 60
1967	InterLisp	Lisp
1967	SNOBOL4	SNOBOL3
1967	XPL	PL/I
1968	ALGOL 68 (UNESCO/IFIP standard)	ALGOL 60
1968	POP-1	COWSEL
1968	DIBOL-8	DIBOL
1968	Forth (concept)	
1968	LOGO	LISP
1968	MAPPER	CRT RPS
1968	REFAL (implementation)	
1968	TTM (implementation)	GAP, GPM
1969	PL/I (implementation)	ALGOL 60, COBOL, FORTRAN
1969	B	BCPL

Year	Language	Predecessor(s)
1969	PPL	
1969	SETL	
1969	TUTOR	
1969	Edinburgh IMP	Algol 60, Autocode, Atlas Autocode

5 THE 1970S

The 1970s saw the major development of programming languages and most of the major language paradigms currently in use were invented during this period.

Additionally, during this period there was considerable debate over the merits of "structured programming". Structured programming is a paradigm which makes use of subroutines and loops rather than using jumps such as the GOTO statement. The aim was to produce clearer code which was easier to follow and maintain.

In 1971, Niklaus Wirth introduced a simple block-structured language called Pascal, designed for computer science education. Although initially designed as a teaching language, variations of Pascal have been used for everything from computer games to embedded systems development.

Pascal requires a certain level of discipline from its programmers as all types, data and subroutines in a Pascal program must be explicitly declared prior to use.

Like the popular languages of the 1950s and 60s, Pascal has undergone a number of developments over the years. There have been derivatives such as Object Pascal, which was designed for object-oriented programming.

Also in 1971, Steve Bourne released sh, or Bourne Shell as it was also known. Bourne Shell was one of the original command languages for the Unix operating system. It is used for automating complex tasks using individual Unix tools. Whilst it is not a traditional programming language, the flexibility of Bourne Shell and the provision of control structures such as IF and FOR makes it worthy of inclusion in this book. Bourne Shell also provides extensive features for running programs and handling their input and output, such as the "pipe", which is used to pass the output of one program to the input of another.

In 1972, the first dedicated object-oriented language, Smalltalk, was developed at Xerox PARC. Smalltalk is a pure object-oriented language – all data are encapsulated as objects and all operations are performed by sending messages to those objects.

This concept of message sending is entirely different to the way that non-object-oriented languages work. Consider for example the operation of outputting an item of information (for example a name). In a non-object-oriented language, this would be achieved by a statement such as –

```
print $name
```

Whereas, in an object-oriented language it would be achieved as follows –

```
$person->printName()
```

In the first example, we are using a generic function print to output the variable $name, whilst in the second we are sending a message to the object instance $person telling it to perform the action printName. An important feature of object-oriented programming is that each object would have its own method to perform the outputting of data. So, for example, the printName method for a Person object and the printAddress method for a House object whilst achieving the same thing would be implemented internally in entirely different ways, which the calling function would have no idea about. This concept of abstraction removes from the programmer the need to worry about the underlying data and just concentrate on the objects themselves.

An influential aspect of Smalltalk was its run-time environment. It was the first language to support a multi-window graphical user interface and its ideas can be seen in modern windowing systems such as Microsoft Windows.

The C language was developed in 1972 by Dennis M. Richie at Bell Laboratories. It is a fairly low-level block structured language, with features such as simple data structures, subroutines, memory pointers and simple I/O facilities. C is seen as a fast and powerful language, but at the expense of being more difficult to read than other languages.

C got its name because; as previously mentioned; its features were derived from an earlier programming language called B.

C is one of the most widely used programming languages of all time and there are very few computer architectures for which a C compiler does not exist.

1978 saw the introduction of Awk, a string-processing language developed at Bell Laboratories. Awk offered powerful regular expression pattern matching and quickly became the language of choice for small Unix data transformation programs.

Also in 1978, the Structured Query Language or SQL was introduced commercially, for managing data in relational database management systems. SQL is based on work undertaken at IBM in the early 1970s for the SEQUEL (Structured English QUEry Language) language and was first commercially released by Relational Software Inc as Oracle V2, followed soon after by an IBM version.

SQL is based on the relational database model described in Edgar F. Codd's 1970 paper "A Relational Model of Data for Large Shared Data Banks" and is the most widely used database language.

Even though SQL became a standard of the American National Standards Institute (ANSI) and International Organization for Standards (ISO) in the late 1980s, there are still differences to the flavours of SQL offered by the various relational database management systems products, due to lack of full compliance with the standard.

The most common operation in SQL is the query, which is performed using the SELECT statement. SELECT retrieves data from one or more tables that matches defined conditions. The tables are linked together by key fields and the returned results can be limited by using conditions.

The example below assumes that there are two tables **Book** and **Author**, which are linked by the key field **AuthorId**. For example, the code below would return the titles of all the books written by a particular author sorted in alphabetical order by the book's title.

```
SELECT Book.Title
FROM Book, Author
WHERE Book.AuthorId = Author.AuthorId
AND Author.Name = "James Steinberg"
ORDER BY Book.Title
```

The above query has no persistent affect on the data in the database; it is simple returning a set of data that matches the conditions given.

There is a subset of the SQL referred to as the Data Manipulation Language, that can be used to insert, update and delete data. The updating and deletion can be conditional using a **WHERE** clause as used in the select query.

Important languages of the 1970s

Year	Language	Predecessor(s)
1970?	Forth (implementation)	
1970	POP-2	POP-1
1970	Pascal	ALGOL 60, ALGOL W
1970	BLISS	ALGOL
1971	KRL	KM, FRL (MIT)
1971	Sue	Pascal, XPL
1972	Smalltalk	Simula 67
1972	PL/M	PL/I, ALGOL, XPL
1972	C	B, BCPL, ALGOL 68
1972	INTERCAL	
1972	Prolog	2-level W-Grammar
1972	SQL	Ingres

Year	Language	Predecessor(s)
1973	COMAL	Pascal, BASIC
1973	ML	
1973	LIS	Pascal, Sue
1973	Speakeasy-3	Speakeasy-2
1974	GRASS	BASIC
1974	BASIC FOUR	Business BASIC
1975	ABC	SETL
1975	Scheme	LISP
1975	Altair BASIC	BASIC
1975	CS-4	ALGOL 68, BLISS, ECL, HAL
1975	Modula	Pascal
1976	Plus	Pascal, Sue
1976	Smalltalk-76	Smalltalk-72
1976	Mesa	ALGOL
1976	SAM76	LISP, TRAC
1976	Ratfor	C, FORTRAN
1976	S	APL, PPL, Scheme
1977	FP	
1977	Bourne Shell (sh)	
1977	Commodore BASIC	Licenced from Microsoft
1977	IDL	Fortran
1977	Standard MUMPS	MUMPS
1977	Icon (concept)	SNOBOL
1977	Green	ALGOL 68, LIS
1977	Red	ALGOL 68, CS-4
1977	Blue	ALGOL 68
1977	Yellow	ALGOL 68
1978?	MATLAB	
1978?	SMALL	Algol60
1978	VisiCalc	
1979	Modula-2	Modula, Mesa

Year	Language	Predecessor(s)
1979	REXX	PL/I, BASIC, EXEC 2
1979	AWK	C, SNOBOL
1979	Icon (implementation)	SNOBOL
1979	Vulcan dBase-II	

6 THE 1980S

The 1980s were a period of consolidation, no new paradigms were invented. Instead, the ideas of the previous decade were elaborated on.

The 1980s also saw advances in programming language implementation. For example, the RISC (Reduced Instruction Set Computing) movement in computer architecture proposed that hardware should be designed for compilers rather than for human assembly programmers.

Modula-2 was released in 1980, although the development began in 1977. It was conceived by Niklaus Wirth as a descendent of Pascal. It had a less rigid syntax than Pascal, allowing programmers to declare variables closer to where they were being used.

Whilst Modula-2 enjoyed some degree of success in the early 1980s, its popularity was limited by the fact that it did not support inheritance and was therefore unable to fully implement the object-oriented paradigm that became popular in the late 1980s.

There was little development of the language during the 1990s, but recently there have been efforts to produce a standardised version of the language, referred to as Modula-2 R10.

Also in 1980, Bjarne Stroustrup produced a number of extensions to C, known as C With Classes. These extensions introduced features to C such as multitasking, dynamic variables and interrupt handling. C With Classes would go on to be renamed C++ before it was commercially released.

1982 saw the foundation of Adobe Systems Inc and the introduction of Postscript. Postscript is a Page Description Language that was originally designed to execute inside a printer with very little memory. It is seen as the language of choice for graphical output.

In 1983, Ada was released. Named in honour of Ada Lovelace, it is a block-structured language that features many object-oriented features. Ada was designed for the US Department of Defence, with the aim of being a reliable language with a Pascal-like syntax.

Ada has been designed for use in large-scale critical systems, such as those used in avionics and space technology. Because of this it includes a number of run-time checks to protect against bugs such as trying to access unallocated memory, buffer overflows and range violations.

In July 1983, the first implementation of C++ was released. C++ is a derivation of C that supports object-oriented programming. The syntax of C++ is similar to C, with extensions to support object-oriented features such as classes and inheritance. C++ was originally an extension of C, but soon developed into a language of its own.

C++ compiles to highly efficient code, so it is often used in high performance application domains such as device drivers, embedded systems and video games.

MATLAB (MATrix LABoratory) was developed by Cleve Moler at the University of New Mexico and first released in 1984. MATLAB is a numerical computing environment which allows the manipulation of matrices and plotting of functions.

An area where MATLAB excels is in the plotting of two and three dimensional graphs based on a function. For example, the following code -

```
% Create a grid of x and y points
points = linspace(-2, 2, 40);
[X, Y] = meshgrid(points, points);

% Define the function Z = f(X,Y)
Z = 2./exp((X-.5).^2+Y.^2)-2./exp((X+.5).^2+Y.^2);

% Create the surface plot using the surf command
figure;
surf(X, Y, Z);
```

will produce this output -

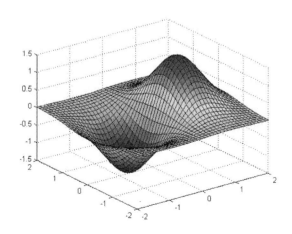

1987 saw the introduction of Perl (Practical Extraction and Reporting Language, which was developed by Larry Wall as a general-purpose Unix scripting language designed for simplifying report processing.

Perl is influenced by a number of languages such as AWK, C, sed and Pascal. Perl became popular for writing Common Gateway Interface scripts and some notable websites such as Amazon.com and the BBC make extensive use of Perl.

Mathematica, which was released in 1988 and designed by Stephen Wolfram is a computational language used in scientific, engineering and mathematical fields.

Mathematica is particularly good at plotting 2D and 3D mathematical functions. For example, the code –

```
Plot3D[Sin[x] Cos[y], {x, 0, 5}, {y, 1, 10}]
```

Will produce the following output –

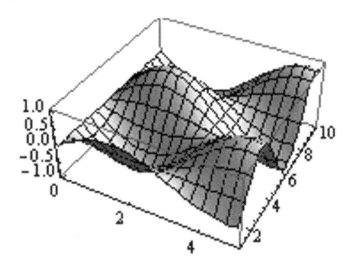

Important languages of the 1980s

Year	Language	Predecessor(s)
1980	Ada 80 (MIL-STD-1815)	Green
1980	C with classes	C, Simula 67
1980–81	CBASIC	BASIC, Compiler Systems, Digital Research
1981	IBM BASICA	BASIC
1982?	Speakeasy-IV	Speakeasy-3
1982?	Draco	Pascal, C, ALGOL 68
1982	PostScript	InterPress
1983	GW-BASIC	IBM BASICA
1983	Ada 83 (ANSI/MIL-STD-1815A)	Ada 80, Green
1983	C++	C with Classes
1983	True BASIC	BASIC
1983	occam	EPL
1983?	ABAP	COBOL
1984	CLIPPER	dBase
1984	Common Lisp	LISP
1984?	GOM – Good Old Mad	MAD
1984?	Korn Shell (ksh)	sh
1984	RPL	Forth, Lisp
1984	Standard ML	ML
1984	Redcode	
1985	PARADOX	dBase
1985	QuickBASIC	BASIC
1986	CorVision	INFORM
1986	Eiffel	Simula 67, Ada
1986	GFA BASIC	BASIC
1986	Informix-4GL	
1986	LabVIEW	
1986	Miranda	
1986	Objective-C	Smalltalk, C

Year	Language	Predecessor(s)
1986	Object Pascal	Pascal
1986	PROMAL	C
1987	Ada ISO 8652:1987	Ada 83
1987	Self (concept)	Smalltalk
1987	occam 2	occam
1987	HyperTalk	
1987	Perl	C, sed, awk, sh
1987	Oberon	Modula-2
1987	Erlang	Prolog
1987	Mathematica	
1987	Turbo Basic	BASIC/Z
1988	Octave	MATLAB
1988	Tcl	Awk, Lisp
1988	STOS BASIC	BASIC
1988	Object REXX	REXX
1988	SPARK	Ada
1988	A+	APL
1989	Turbo Pascal OOP	Turbo Pascal, Object Pascal
1989	Modula-3	Modula-2
1989	PowerBASIC	Turbo Basic
1989	VisSim	
1989	LPC	

7 THE 1990S

The 1990s was the decade of the Internet and many of the developments that took place during the decade were driven by the needs of the new technology.

Also during this decade, many Rapid Application Development (RAD) languages emerged. These languages were descendents of older languages and were object-oriented. There was also a move to scripted languages within larger applications, such as the use of VBA (Visual Basic for Applications) within the MS Office suite. These scripted languages are used for automation of tasks within the applications.

In 1991, the Java language project was initiated and the language was finally released in 1995 by Sun Microsystems. All data and methods within Java are associated with a class.

Applications that are written in Java are compiled to bytecode that can then run on any Java virtual machine regardless of the underlying computer architecture. Java became very popular due to its early integration with the Netscape Navigator web browser.

Java software runs on platforms from mobile phones, games consoles, all the way through to supercomputers.

A further introduction in 1991 was the first version of Visual Basic from Microsoft. The visual element of Visual Basic referred to its Integrated Development Environment, which has extensive facilities for the design of dialog boxes, menus and other windows interfaces.

One of the reasons for Visual Basic's popularity is that it is similar in syntax to most other modern Basic dialects, but includes a number of additional features. Many computer professionals of the early 1990s cut their programming teeth using the versions of Basic included with their Sinclair, Atari and Commodore home computers from a decade before, so Visual Basic was immediately familiar to them.

Although not a programming language per se (it is as its name suggests a markup language), HTML is an important language in the development of the World Wide Web. HTML controls the display of text and graphics in a web browser.

HTML is written using HTML elements that consist of tags enclosed in angle brackets, within the web page content. The tags are used by web browsers such as Internet Explorer, Firefox, Google Chrome and Apple Safari to format the output of the webpage, such as defining headings or displaying images.

HTML was specified in 1991 by British physicist Tim Berners-Lee at CERN in Switzerland as a means of linking documents together using hypertext links.

JavaScript was introduced in 1994, initially as LiveScript by Netscape. Sun Microsystems took an interest in the script and worked with Netscape to improve it and release it as JavaScript.

JavaScript is primarily used as a client-side scripting language in web browsers and has extensive facilities for manipulating and controlling the content of web pages. For example, it is often used as a means of enabling parts of a web page to be hidden until some action takes place, such as displaying a drop-down sub-menu when a menu item is rolled over. Another popular use is validating the content of forms before they are submitted to a web server.

In 1995, the first public version of Ruby was announced. It is a fully object-oriented language where all data types are object classes. Ruby has a simple syntax that is similar to that of Perl and is also influenced by Eiffel and Lisp.

Another product of the Web boom, PHP was also introduced in 1995 as a server-side scripting language for the production of dynamic Web pages. PHP is an open source language and was one of the first server-side scripting languages that could be embedded directly into an HTML document. PHP is very popular with web developers and is estimated to be installed on in excess of 20 million web sites.

Because PHP is a server-side language, the PHP source file is executed by the PHP runtime on the server and usually generates an HTML file for display in the web page visitor's browser. PHP is often teamed with a relational database management system such as MySQL to enable it to generate web pages based on the contents of the database. This approach is used in sites such as ecommerce and forums.

VB Script, which was first released with Microsoft's Internet Explorer 3.0 in 1997, is a general-purpose scripting language that is a subset of Visual Basic.

VB Script was initially designed as a tool for web developers and was Microsoft's answer to the popular JavaScript scripting language used by Netscape in its web browser. Its popularity and use has spread though and it is used for automation purposes in a number of applications, such as the Quick Test Professional test automation tool.

Important languages of the 1990s

Year	Language	Predecessor(s)
1990	AMOS BASIC	STOS BASIC
1990	AMPL	
1990	Object Oberon	Oberon
1990	J	APL, FP
1990	Haskell	Miranda
1990	EuLisp	Common Lisp, Scheme
1990	Z Shell (zsh)	ksh
1991	GNU E	C++
1991	Oberon-2	Object Oberon
1991	Python	ABC, ALGOL 68, Icon, Modula-3
1991	Oz	Prolog
1991	Q	
1991	Visual Basic	QuickBASIC
1992	Borland Pascal	Turbo Pascal OOP
1992	Dylan	Common Lisp, Scheme
1993?	Self (implementation)	Smalltalk
1993	Brainf}ck	P"
1993	FALSE	Forth
1993	Revolution Transcript	HyperTalk
1993	AppleScript	HyperTalk
1993	K	APL, Lisp
1993	Lua	Scheme, SNOBOL, Modula, CLU, C++

Year	Language	Predecessor(s)
1993	R	S
1993	ZPL	C
1993	NewtonScript	Self, Dylan
1994	ANSI Common Lisp	Common Lisp
1994	RAPID	ARLA
1994	Pike	LPC, C, μLPC
1994	ANS Forth	Forth
1995	Ada 95	Ada 83
1995	Borland Delphi	Borland Pascal
1995	ColdFusion (CFML)	
1995	Java	C, Simula 67, C++, Smalltalk, Ada 83, Objective-C, Mesa
1995	LiveScript	Self, C, Scheme
1995	PHP	Perl
1995	Ruby	Smalltalk, Perl
1996	Curl	Lisp, C++, Tcl/Tk, TeX, HTML
1996	JavaScript	LiveScript
1996	Perl Data Language (PDL)	APL, Perl
1996	NetRexx	REXX
1996	Lasso	
1997	Component Pascal	Oberon-2
1997	E	Joule, Original-E
1997	Pico	Scheme
1997	Squeak Smalltalk	Smalltalk-80, Self
1997	ECMAScript	JavaScript
1997	F-Script	Smalltalk, APL, Objective-C
1997	ISLISP	Common Lisp
1997	Tea	Java, Scheme, Tcl
1997	REBOL	Self, Forth, Lisp, Logo

Year	Language	Predecessor(s)
1998	Standard C++	C++, Standard C, C
1998	Open Source Erlang	Erlang
1998	M2001	*
1998	Pikt	AWK, Perl, Unix shell
1998	PureBasic	
1999	XSLT (+ XPath)	DSSSL
1999	Game Maker Language (GML)	Game Maker
1999	Harbour	dBase

8 THE 2000S AND BEYOND

The new millennium has seen a continued evolution in programming languages, with trends such as functional programming, distributed programming and massively parallel languages. There has also been evolution in the support for Unicode in source code to allow the development of non-Latin-based scripts and extended punctuation.

Another innovation that the new millennium has bought about is what devices we are programming for. In the early days of programming, the programs were written to run on room-sized computers. The present has seen the introduction of tablets and smart phones with processing power far in excess of what the early computer pioneers could ever have dreamed of. With these devices has come a whole new industry, with developers specialising in the development of 'apps' for these new devices.

There have also been a number of new languages introduced during the period.

ActionScript was introduced in 2000 by Macromedia Inc, who are now a part of Adobe Systems. ActionScript was developed as a language for controlling 2D vector animations created in Macromedia Flash. It is an open-source object-oriented scripting language and has gone through a number of versions, which have added features such as 3D graphics capabilities.

Released in 2001 by Microsoft as part of their .Net initiative, C♯ (C Sharp) is intended to be a simple, general purpose object-oriented language.

C Sharp has been defined by a number of people in the programming community as being an "imitation of" or "almost identical to" Java. However, since the release of C♯ 2.0, the languages have started to become less similar and began to evolve in increasingly different directions.

Another element of Microsoft's .Net initiative also released in 2001 was Visual Basic .Net. VB .Net is an evolution of the earlier Visual Basic and it is a subject of debate in programming circles as to whether it is new language or just a new version of the earlier language. My personal opinion is that it is a version of VB, which seems to be backed up by Microsoft's versioning of it, which started with version 7. It is however a significant enough evolution to have a place in the history of programming languages.

Initially discussed in 2003 and first released in 2007, Groovy is an object-oriented language that can be used as a scripting language for the Java platform. It is similar to languages such as Python, Ruby and Perl. Because Groovy compiles to Java Virtual Machine bytecode, it is architecture independent and a compiled file will run on different machines without further effort being required.

Showing the power and diversity of the Web-based corporations, Google Inc released the Go language in 2009, with compilers for a number of popular operating systems. The language is syntactically broadly similar to that of C, with some differences such as not needing semi-colons at the end of each line. Although developed by Google, Go is an open source project.

Another of Google's developments is the Dart language introduced in 2011. Dart has been designed to replace JavaScript as the unifying language of web development. Dart is another C-style object-oriented language.

The main perceived problem with Dart is that it is currently not supported in Internet Explorer, Firefox, Opera and Safari browsers, so there is a real risk of websites being developed that only work properly in Google's Chrome browser.

Important languages of the 2000s and beyond

Year	Language	Predecessor(s)
2000	Join Java	Java
2000	ActionScript	ECMAScript
2000	Joy	FP, Forth
2000	D	C, C++, C#, Java
2000	XL	Ada, C++, Lisp
2000	C♯	C, C++, Java, Delphi, Modula-2
2000	Ferite	C, C++, Java, PHP, Python, Ruby, Scheme
2001	AspectJ	Java, Common Lisp
2001	Processing	*
2001	Visual Basic .NET	Visual Basic
2002	Io	Self, NewtonScript
2003	Nemerle	C#, ML, MetaHaskell

Year	Language	Predecessor(s)
2003	Factor	Joy, Forth, Lisp
2003	Scala	Smalltalk, Java, Haskell, Standard ML, OCaml
2003	Squirrel	Lua
2004	Subtext	*
2004	Alma-0	*
2004	Boo	Python, C#
2004	FreeBASIC	QBasic
2004	Groovy	Java
2004	Little b	Lisp
2005	F#	Objective Caml, C#, Haskell
2005	Seed7	*
2006	Links	Haskell
2006	Cobra	Python, C#, Eiffel, Objective-C
2006	Windows PowerShell	C#, ksh, Perl, CL, DCL, SQL
2006	OptimJ	Java
2007	Ada 2005	Ada 95
2007	Fantom	C#, Scala, Ruby, Erlang
2007	Vala	C#
2007	Clojure	Lisp, ML, Haskell, Erlang
2007	Fortress	Scala, ML, Haskell
2007	Oberon-07	Oberon
2008	Genie	Python, Boo, D, Object Pascal
2008	Pure	Q
2009	Go	C, Oberon, Limbo
2009	CoffeeScript	JavaScript, Ruby, Python, Haskell
2010	Fancy	Smalltalk, Ruby, Io, Erlang
2010	Grace	*

Year	Language	Predecessor(s)
2010	Rust	Alef, C++, Camlp4, Common Lisp, Erlang, Hermes, Limbo, Napier, Napier88, Newsqueak, NIL, Sather, Standard ML
2010	Kotlin	Java
2011	Dart	Java, JavaScript, CoffeeScript, Go
2011	Ceylon	Java
2012	TypeScript	JavaScript, CoffeeScript

9 THE FUTURE

I obviously don't have a crystal ball or a time machine, so it is not possible to give a definite statement as to the future of programming, but here are some predictions of how things may develop (if you pardon the pun).

'Smart devices' will continue to diversify – already, there are smart watches that interact with the owner's smart phone to display emails, texts and tweets. These will continue to evolve and as they do, so will the programming languages used to write the apps that run on them.

Programming will also likely continue to move away from the realm of the specialist who is employed to just write programs. Scripting facilities within applications such as MS Office and Open Office already mean that non-programmers can produce small programs or modules to automate repetitive tasks themselves rather than waiting for a solution to be produced by their company's development team.

At a recent conference I spoke to an actuarial manager working for a large insurance company, who told me that he had got fed up with waiting for a formal project to be raised every time he needed to make changes to the scripts behind his Excel spreadsheets. His solution is that he will be sending some of the more IT minded members of his team on a course to train them in the basics of Visual Basic for Applications.

No doubt many of the languages currently in use will continue to evolve with added features and changes in direction. There will also be new languages introduced to support as yet unknown evolutions in computing hardware and unthought-of devices.

Another area which is likely to have an affect on the future of programming is the continuing growth in the importance of data. Modern languages tend to focus on the object-oriented paradigm where data is wrapped up in to classes with access methods. In the statistical world data has no behaviour and does not fit neatly into classes, yet object-oriented languages force developers to take this approach. This could lead to more simplistic languages that treat data as data rather than forcing it in to an un-necessary class.

10 PUNCHED CARDS TO PCS

This chapter is based on the memories of two programmers. The first is my uncle Richard Steinberg, who gives an insight into the programming of computers in the early 1970s. The second is one of my students Ian Mugridge, who is a modern day programmer.

Programming in the 1970s

I started working for IBM in the late 60s and in the spring of 1972, took up a new role as a junior programmer. I was assigned an office which I shared with 2 experienced programmers. The first thing that struck me was the number of boxes that they had stored in the room. Each of these boxes stored around 2000 of the punched cards upon which a program was written.

The process of writing and then running a program was quite a complicated one. The first thing that the programmer had to do was write their program on a series of coding forms similar to the one shown on the next page. Each coding form had about fifty lines on it and each line would eventually be transformed into a punched card representing that particular line of code.

The programming process involved writing and amending the code on the coding forms until you were happy with it, then you could move on to the next stage.

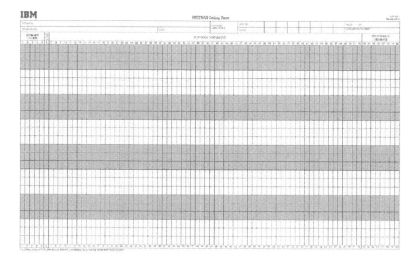

Once the programmer had their completed program written on the coding sheets, they would take it to the keypunch operator and leave it with them. The keypunch operator would use a keypunch machine to transfer each line of code on the coding sheets to an individual punched card. Each punched card would have the code punched into it and also the code itself typed at the top of the card, similar to that shown below.

Once the programmer had his stack of punched cards, the next stage was to check that they had been punched correctly. This involved going through the stack a card at a time and comparing the code typed at the top with the corresponding line on the coding forms.

This stack of cards contained the program I had written in the language I had used (FORTRAN), but it was not actually able to run on the computer. This stack was the source stack and had to be processed by the computer using a program called a compiler to produce the runable program card stack.

So, the next stage is to take your source stack to the computer room for it to be run through the compiler. Junior programmers weren't allowed in the computer room, that was the domain of the computer operator. Instead, the programmer took his stack of cards to the 'in tray' of the computer room and filled out a request form. Then you went away and waited.

In the computer room, a computer operator will take the next stack of cards from the 'in tray' and put them into the computer's punched card reader, which is connected to the computer. The computer in this case was an IBM 360, which was made up of various components (console, tape storage, card reader, printer, etc.) and took up a fair amount of the room. The punched card reader reads the cards and passes the instructions to the computer to process.

Once the compiler program has run, the source cards, the program output (on a stack of printer paper) and (hopefully) the outputted program punched cards would be collated together by the computer operator. These would then be put in the computer room's 'out tray' for the programmer to collect.

Once the programmer has received his output back from the computer room he would need to review it. There are two likely scenarios. The first is that the output would include a stack of program cards, indicating that the program had compiled successfully. The other is that there are no program cards, which would indicate that the program had failed to compile and there was a problem with the source punched cards.

If the compiler had failed to compile the program then the programmer would need to find the errors and fix it. This would involve searching through the source looking for the error (often something as simple as a missing comma) and then completing a coding form to enable a replacement punched card to be created. The punched cards could then be resubmitted to the computer room for processing. This process would be repeated until the program compiles and the stack of program punched cards are created.

Once the program punched cards have been created, you are then in a position to run your own program, so it is back to the computer room. The programmer would submit his program punched cards and a request form and wait for the program to be run.

Once the program had run, the punched cards and the printed output would be put in the computer room's 'out' tray to be collected by the programmer. Then the fun really began.

Having got his printed output back, the programmer would start by looking to see if the outputted results were as expected. If, as was likely, they weren't it was an indication that the program had errors (or bugs) in it and would need to be debugged. This was done by manually working through the source code on the compiler program's output, to work out where the program was going wrong. When the source of the error was found, the source code was marked up with the corrections that needed to be made. These corrections were then copied onto a coding form and taken to the keypunch operator to get new punched cards produced to replace the errors.

The punched cards would then be taken back to the computer room to be run through the compiler and the re-compiled program would then be run again. This process would be completed time and time again until the output was as expected.

This process could take days or even weeks for a reasonable sized program; due to the fact that contention for the computer resource between the various programmers limited the number of times you could run the program to perhaps half a dozen times a day.

There was also another problem with this constant re-compiling and re-running of the program. The source punched cards were constantly being handled by the programmer and put through the card reader. This caused a lot of wear and tear on the cards and eventually the reader would not be able to read the damaged cards. This meant that the source cards had to be replaced with a new set. This was done by going back to the keypunch operator and asking them to run the old cards through a punched card duplicator to produce a new set of identical cards.

Programming in the 2000s

I have worked as a C developer for a number of companies since I left university. I am currently working for a small consultancy company who work on data migrations for financial services organisations. I work in a largely 'paperless' office with all of the information about the program I am writing being stored on the hard drives of the company's server. I am one of a team of three developers and one or more of us may be working on a program at a particular time.

The development of a program is based on analysis done by the company's team of Business Analysts, who will produce pseudo-code to define how individual parts of the program will function. It is from this pseudo-code that the actual program code will be written.

The programs that we write are large and as mentioned previously, will have a number of developers working on them at the same time. The program is divided into a number of source files, which are all saved separately and to avoid conflicts, only one developer will work on a particular source file at a time.

The master copies of the source files are stored on the company's server (which is in the head office 20 miles from where I am based and is connected over a leased line) and are controlled by a version control system. When a developer wants to work on a particular file he will 'check it out', which copies a version onto his local machine. In my case, that local machine is a Dell laptop running the Windows NT operating system.

The writing of the program code is done using a text editor on the laptop and once I have written the code, I will save it and then check it back in to the master copy. I then sit down with the Business Analyst and we undertake a code walkthrough to compare my code to their pseudo-code and ensure they are doing the same thing.

After the code walkthrough, I use the version control system to release the code onto the machine on which it will be running. This machine will normally belong to the client that we are working on and can be located anywhere and connected to again via leased lines. The machines are often running a flavour of Unix operating system.

When all the code has been released, it will be compiled on the remote machine and can then be run. This is all achieved using a remote shell connection from my laptop to the client's machine and working in Unix.

Once the program has run and assuming that it didn't crash then the results will be passed to the Business Analyst to compare against their expected results.

If the program crashed or the results are not as expected then the program will need to be debugged. This is done using a debugger such as gdb. The debugger will be launched and a breakpoint can be set at a particular line or function within the C program. The program is then executed from within the debugger and will run normally until it gets to the breakpoint. Once the program is at the breakpoint, it is possible to view the value of variables or step through the code a line at a time.

Once the bugs have been identified, the code is updated on the local machine, checked back in to the master copy and then released back on to the target machine. The code can then be compiled and run again and checked for errors. This process is repeated until the results are as expected.

A comparison of 1970s and 2000s programming

Having read Richard and Ian's accounts of programming in their respective decades, it is useful to consider the differences between the way the job was performed over 30 years apart.

Feature	1970s	2000s
People involved	Programmer, keypunch operator and computer operator.	Developers.
Equipment involved	A keypunch machine, a card reader, an IBM 360 computer and a line printer.	A laptop, servers and leased line connections.
Storage of program source	Stored on punched cards, which would be kept by the programmer in his office.	Stored as source files on the company's server.
Version control	Limited – changes were made and the old punched cards usually thrown away.	Full version control using a system such as CVS.
Timescales	Days or weeks	Hours or days

11 EVOLUTION OF A LANGUAGE

FORTRAN was the first high level language to be released in the late 1950s and had its most recent version released in 2008. The language has evolved as new versions have been released and this chapter shows the differences between some of the versions.

We will use an algorithm called the Trabb Pardo–Knuth algorithm, which was specifically designed to show the evolution of programming languages. The algorithm reads 11 numbers from an input device, reverses the order and then applies a user defined function (in this case $\sqrt{x} + 5 * x^3$) to each value and displays the output from the function or a message if the value exceeds a threshold.

FORTRAN

```
        DIMENSION A(11)
        READ A
2       DO 3,8,11 J=1,11
3       I=11-J
        Y=SQRT(ABS(A(I+1)))+5*A(I+1)**3
        IF (400>=Y) 8,4
4       PRINT I,999.
        GOTO 2
8       PRINT I,Y
11      STOP
```

The original version of FORTRAN was not able to output text; therefore the value 999 is used to indicate numbers that were too large.

FORTRAN II

```
C       THE TPK ALGORITHM
        FUNF(T)=SQRTF(ABSF(T))+5.0*T**3
        DIMENSION A(11)
1       FORMAT(6F12.4)
        READ 1,A
        DO 10 J=1,11
        I=11-J
        Y=FUNF(A(I+1))
        IF(400.0-Y)4,8,8
4       PRINT 5,I
5       FORMAT(I10,10H TOO LARGE)
        GOTO 10
8       PRINT 9,I,Y
9       FORMAT(I10,F12.7)
10      CONTINUE
        STOP 52525
```

FORTRAN II was the first language to allow comments. The reverse DO loop has to be simulated as this version did not allow negative indexes in the loops.

FORTRAN IV/Fortran 66

```
C       THE TPK ALGORITHM
        DIMENSION A(11)
        FUN(T) = SQRT(ABS(T)) + 5.)*T**3
        READ (5,1) A
1       FORMAT(5F10.2)
        DO 10 J = 1, 11
          I = 11 - J
          Y = FUN(A(I+1))
          IF (400.0-Y) 4, 8, 8
4             WRITE (6,5) I
5             FORMAT(I10, 10H TOO LARGE)
          GO TO 10
8             WRITE(6,9) I, Y
              FORMAT(I10, F12.6)
10      CONTINUE
        STOP
        END
```

In this version, again the backwards loop is simulated, but a more structured layout is used. Use is still made of a GOTO statement to allow flow control in the IF statement.

Fortran 77

```
         PROGRAM TPK
C        THE TPK ALGORITHM
         REAL A(0:10)
         READ (5,*) A
         DO 10 I = 10, 0, -1
             Y = FUN(A(I))
             IF ( Y . LT. 400) THEN
                 WRITE(6,9) I,Y
9                FORMAT(I10. F12.6)
             ELSE
                 WRITE (6,5) I
5                FORMAT(I10,' TOO LARGE')
             ENDIF
10       CONTINUE
         END

         REAL FUNCTION FUN(T)
         REAL T
         FUN = SQRT(ABS(T)) + 5.0*T**3
         END
```

Here the program is taking a more modern structure. The simulated backwards loop is no longer needed, as decreasing indexes are supported. The need for a GOTO statement has also been removed with the introduction of an IF THEN ELSE structure.

FORTRAN 90

```fortran
              PROGRAM TPK
!             The TPK Algorithm
              IMPLICIT NONE
              INTEGER                    :: I
              REAL                       :: Y
              REAL, DIMENSION(0:10) :: A
              READ (*,*) A
              DO I = 10, 0, -1              ! Backwards
                  Y = FUN(A(I))
                  IF ( Y < 400.0 ) THEN
                      WRITE(*,*) I, Y
                  ELSE
                      WRITE(*,*) I, ' Too large'
                  END IF
              END DO
              CONTAINS                  ! Local function
                  FUNCTION FUN(T)
                  REAL :: FUN
                  REAL, INTENT(IN) :: T
                  FUN = SQRT(ABS(T)) + 5.0*T**3
                  END FUNCTION FUN
              END PROGRAM TPK
```

Again, the decreasing index in the loop is supported and the loop now ends with an END DO statement rather than a CONTINUE statement. The line numbers have also been removed, giving a contemporary feel. Finally, comments are now marked with an ! and can appear on the same line as a statement.

12 AN ALTERNATIVE HISTORY

While surfing the Web looking for information for a lecture I came across the following humorous alternative history of programming. The article was mainly written by James Iry on his blog http://james-iry.blogspot as A Brief, Incomplete, and Mostly Wrong History of Programming Languages. Additional portions are by Dave Mason.

1801 - Joseph Marie Jacquard uses punch cards to instruct a loom to weave "hello, world" into a tapestry. Redditers of the time are not impressed due to the lack of tail call recursion, concurrency, or proper capitalization.

1842 - Ada Lovelace writes the first program. She is hampered in her efforts by the minor inconvenience that she doesn't have any actual computers to run her code. Enterprise architects will later relearn her techniques in order to program in UML.

1936 - Alan Turing invents every programming language that will ever be but is shanghaied by British Intelligence to be 007 before he can patent them.

1936 - Alonzo Church also invents every language that will ever be but does it better. His lambda calculus is ignored because it is insufficiently C-like. This criticism occurs in spite of the fact that C has not yet been invented.

1940s - Various "computers" are "programmed" using direct wiring and switches. Engineers do this in order to avoid the tabs vs spaces debate.

1957 - John Backus and IBM create FORTRAN. There's nothing funny about IBM or FORTRAN. It is a syntax error to write FORTRAN while not wearing a blue tie.

1958 - John McCarthy and Paul Graham invent LISP. Due to high costs caused by a post-war depletion of the strategic parentheses reserve LISP never becomes popular. In spite of its lack of popularity, LISP (now "Lisp" or sometimes "Arc") remains an influential language in "key algorithmic techniques such as recursion and condescension".

1959 - After losing a bet with L. Ron Hubbard, Grace Hopper and several other sadists invent the Capitalization Of Boilerplate Oriented Language (COBOL) . Years later, in a misguided and sexist retaliation against Adm. Hopper's COBOL work, Ruby conferences frequently feature misogynistic material.

1964 - John Kemeny and Thomas Kurtz create BASIC, an unstructured programming language for non-computer scientists.

1965 - Kemeny and Kurtz go to 1964.

1970 - Guy Steele and Gerald Sussman create Scheme. Their work leads to a series of "Lambda the Ultimate" papers culminating in "Lambda the Ultimate Kitchen Utensil." This paper becomes the basis for a long running, but ultimately unsuccessful run of late night infomercials. Lambdas are relegated to relative obscurity until Java makes them popular by not having them.

1970 - Niklaus Wirth creates Pascal, a procedural language. Critics immediately denounce Pascal because it uses "x := x + y" syntax instead of the more familiar C-like "x = x + y". This criticism happens in spite of the fact that C has not yet been invented.

1972 - Dennis Ritchie invents a powerful gun that shoots both forward and backward simultaneously. Not satisfied with the number of deaths and permanent maimings from that invention he invents C and Unix.

1972 - Alain Colmerauer designs the logic language Prolog. His goal is to create a language with the intelligence of a two year old. He proves he has reached his goal by showing a Prolog session that says "No." to every query.

1973 - Robin Milner creates ML, a language based on the M&M type theory. ML begets SML which has a formally specified semantics. When asked for a formal semantics of the formal semantics Milner's head explodes. Other well known languages in the ML family include OCaml, F#, and Visual Basic.

1980 - Alan Kay creates Smalltalk and invents the term "object oriented." When asked what that means he replies, "Smalltalk programs are just objects." When asked what objects are made of he replies, "objects." When asked again he says "look, it's all objects all the way down. Until you reach turtles."

1983 - In honour of Ada Lovelace's ability to create programs that never ran, Jean Ichbiah and the US Department of Defense create the Ada programming language. In spite of the lack of evidence that any significant Ada program is ever completed historians believe Ada to be a successful public works project that keeps several thousand roving defence contractors out of gangs.

1983 - Bjarne Stroustrup bolts everything he's ever heard of onto C to create C++. The resulting language is so complex that programs must be sent to the future to be compiled by the Skynet artificial intelligence. Build times suffer. Skynet's motives for performing the service remain unclear but spokespeople from the future say "there is nothing to be concerned about, baby," in an Austrian accented monotones. There is some speculation that Skynet is nothing more than a pretentious buffer overrun.

1986 - Brad Cox and Tom Love create Objective-C, announcing "this language has all the memory safety of C combined with all the blazing speed of Smalltalk." Modern historians suspect the two were dyslexic.

1986 - Since concurrency programming was so obscure and difficult, Joe Armstrong invented Erlang because a little Prolog syntax and Lisp semantics was bound to make things clearer.

1987 - Larry Wall falls asleep and hits Larry Wall's forehead on the keyboard. Upon waking Larry Wall decides that the string of characters on Larry Wall's monitor isn't random but an example program in a programming language that God wants His prophet, Larry Wall, to design. Perl is born.

1990 - A committee formed by Simon Peyton-Jones, Paul Hudak, Philip Wadler, Ashton Kutcher, and People for the Ethical Treatment of Animals creates Haskell, a pure, non-strict, functional language. Haskell gets some resistance due to the complexity of using monads to control side effects. Wadler tries to appease critics by explaining that "a monad is a monoid in the category of endofunctors, what's the problem?"

1991 - Dutch programmer Guido van Rossum travels to Argentina for a mysterious operation. He returns with a large cranial scar, invents Python, is declared Dictator for Life by legions of followers, and announces to the world that "There Is Only One Way to Do It." Poland becomes nervous.

1995 - At a neighborhood Italian restaurant Rasmus Lerdorf realizes that his plate of spaghetti is an excellent model for understanding the World Wide Web and that web applications should mimic their medium. On the back of his napkin he designs Programmable Hyperlinked Pasta (PHP). PHP documentation remains on that napkin to this day.

1995 - Yukihiro "Mad Matz" Matsumoto creates Ruby to avert some vaguely unspecified apocalypse that will leave Australia a desert run by mohawked warriors and Tina Turner. The language is later renamed Ruby on Rails by its real inventor, David Heinemeier Hansson.

1995 - Brendan Eich reads up on every mistake ever made in designing a programming language, invents a few more, and creates LiveScript. Later, in an effort to cash in on the popularity of Java the language is renamed JavaScript. Later still, in an effort to cash in on the popularity of skin diseases the language is renamed ECMAScript.

1996 - James Gosling invents Java. Java is a relatively verbose, garbage collected, class based, statically typed, single dispatch, object oriented language with single implementation inheritance and multiple interface inheritance. Sun loudly heralds Java's novelty.

2001 - Anders Hejlsberg invents C#. C# is a relatively verbose, garbage collected, class based, statically typed, single dispatch, object oriented language with single implementation inheritance and multiple interface inheritance. Microsoft loudly heralds C#'s novelty.

2002 - Because Smalltalk had too many constructs and was too mainstream, Steve Dekorte invented Io.

2003 - A drunken Martin Odersky sees a Reese's Peanut Butter Cup ad featuring somebody's peanut butter getting on somebody else's chocolate and has an idea. He creates Scala, a language that unifies constructs from both object oriented and functional languages. This pisses off both groups and each promptly declares jihad.

2008 - Rich Hickey turned Clojure loose on the world because he found a new supplier of parentheses and thought they'd make Haskell more approachable.

13 PROGRAMMING PARADIGMS

A programming paradigm can be thought of as a school of thought for programming. There are four recognised main programming paradigms and a number of minor paradigms.

The four main paradigms are –

- Imperative
- Functional
- Logical
- Object-oriented

Imperative programming is defined by the fact that they are based on a series of statements that change a program's state. An example of a statement in an imperative program is –

```
x := x + 1
```

The earliest forms of imperative language can be considered to be machine code and assembly language. Other examples of imperative languages are Fortran, Pascal, Basic and C.

Functional programming treats the program as the evaluation of mathematical functions. In a pure functional language a mathematical identity like:

fred(x) + fred(x) = 2*fred(x)

should hold true.

Functional programming tends to be centred more in academia than in commercial enterprises, although some languages such as Common Lisp and Scala have been used commercially.

Logical programming is based on axioms, queries and inference rules, with a basic concept of the relation. For example consider how brother can be defined in relation to father and mother, using Prolog syntax –

```
brother(X,Y)    /* X is the brother of Y              */
  :-            /* if there are two people F and M for which*/
  father(F,X),  /*      F is the father of X           */
  father(F,Y),  /*  and F is the father of Y           */
  mother(M,X),/*  and M is the mother of X           */
  mother(M,Y),/*  and M is the mother of Y           */
```

Examples of logical programming languages are Prolog and Datalog.

Object-oriented programming focuses on objects that have attributes (data fields) and methods (procedures). In pure object-oriented programming all access to an object's attributes is done through a corresponding method. For example, if an object had a **Name** attribute then it would also have **getName()** and **setName()** methods to access the name data.

An object is an instance of a class and there will normally be many instances of a particular class when a program runs. For example if there is a customer class then there will be a separate object instance to represent each customer.

Classes are normally arranged into a hierarchy that represents a "kind-of" relationship. For example, if we consider the implementation of a School model, which might have a **person** class to represent the various people associated with the school. There might be sub-classes of **person** called **student** and **teacher**. Both students and teachers will share behaviours (methods) and attributes applicable to people, such as walking, talking, sleeping, name and date of birth. However, the sub-classes will have their own unique behaviours – for example, a teacher will teach and a student will have test marks.

The object-oriented paradigm is supported at a number of levels by different programming languages –

- There are pure object-oriented languages, such as Ruby, Scala and Smalltalk. These are languages that have been designed specifically to use (or even enforce) object-oriented methodologies.
- Then there are languages that have been designed for object-oriented programming, but have some procedural elements. Examples of these languages are Java, C♯ and VB.NET.
- Finally, there are procedural languages that have been extended with some object-oriented features, such as Visual Basic and PHP.

14 ESOTERIC PROGRAMMING LANGUAGES

The vast majority of programming languages are produced either to be released commercially or to meet a specific requirement. There is however a growing Internet community of people creating languages just for fun or for a joke. These languages are known as esoteric programming languages.

The earliest known deliberate esoteric programming language is INTERCALC, which was designed in 1972. The number of esoteric languages being developed took off in the early 1990s when the Internet became popular, giving hobby programmers a means with which to challenge each other and develop languages of their own.

There are a number of different reasons for creating an esoteric programming language, but five common reasons are –

- Minimalism – to design a language that has as few instructions as possible, but still be a working language. An example of this type of language is Brainf!ck.
- Weirdness – to design a language that is difficult to program in, for example Malbolge.

- New concepts – to design a language in an alternative way to the norm. An example of this is Befunge.
- Themed – to design a language with a theme that is not computer related. Examples of this are Shakespeare, whose programs look like Shakespearean plays and Chef, where the programs look like recopies.
- Jokes – some languages are just designed as a joke, often not even being usable for programming. An example of this is the Hello language, which has just one instruction 'h', which displays the text "Hello, World!".

15 DEBUGGING – LITERALLY!

Anyone who has been involved in the computer industry will likely be aware that errors in programs are referred to as bugs and that removing them is referred to as debugging. What they may not be aware of though is how these names came about.

The use of the term "bug" to define a defect predates computers and software and may originally have been used in hardware engineering to describe mechanical malfunctions or problems.

During the Second World War, problems with radar electronics were also referred to as bugs.

However, there is evidence that its usage goes further back than that. An example of its use was by Thomas Edison in an 1878 letter to an associate where he described the faults inherent in his inventions:

It has been just so in all of my inventions. The first step is an intuition, and comes with a burst, then difficulties arise — this thing gives out and [it is] then that "Bugs" — as such little faults and difficulties are called — show themselves and months of intense watching, study and labor are requisite before commercial success or failure is certainly reached.

The terms gathered more of a meaning in the computer world in 1947, when operators at the Computation Laboratory of Harvard traced an error in their Mark II computer to a moth trapped in a relay. Their entry in the computer's log included the sentence "First actual case of bug being found".

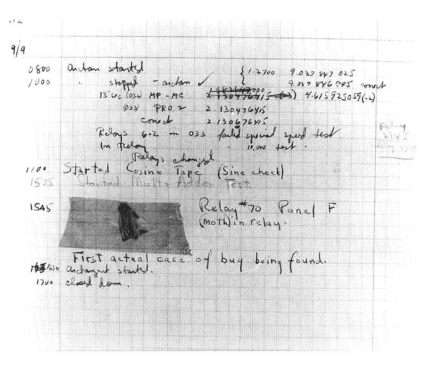

In the early years of modern computers, debugging was a very hit-or-miss procedure and involved either data dumps of the system or output devices to indicate that an error had occurred. The programmer would then step through the code line by line until they traced the error.

As computers developed, so did debugging. The first development was the introduction of command-line debuggers. These allowed a programmer to directly look at the registers and memory blocks that held local variables.

When the higher level languages were developed, developers realised that they could map memory addresses to variable names and to dump the memory by name. These were called symbolic debuggers after the symbol map file in which the additional mapping information was stored.

The next big step in debugging was the ability to set breakpoints in the code. Before breakpoint development, the programmer was only aware of two states of the program – the initial state before it ran and the final state after it finished running. With breakpoints, it was possible to stop the code at a particular line and view the state of the program at that time.

Initially, it was only possible to stop the program at a given line of code. Soon, however, conditional breakpoints were introduced. This allowed the code execution to be halted when a given condition was met (such as a variable being equal to 0).

Up until this time, debugging had been undertaken separately from development, using separate utilities. The next development in debugging was the introduction of the Integrated Development Environment (IDE), which allowed developers to edit, compile, link and debug code in the same system. These IDEs continued to be developed and when from simple text based systems to the fully-fledged GUI based systems such as Visual C++ that you see today.

16 "HELLO, WORLD!" TRANSLATED

When first starting programming in a new language, a common first program is Hello World, which in its most basic form does nothing more than output the string "Hello, World!". This small program provides an ideal source for the comparison of the various languages that are available.

This chapter provides an implementation of the Hello World program in a number of popular, archaic and joke/esoteric languages from the history of programming languages.

Assembly Language

Assembly language is a low-level programming language where each instruction corresponds to a single machine code instruction. The assembly language program is converted into machine code for execution using a utility called an assembler.

Assembly language has been around since the late 1940s and is still in use today in modern computers.

Different computer architectures have different versions of assembly language with differences in the mnemonics used.

6502 Commodore 64 Assembler

; Hello World for 6502 Assembler (C64)

```
ldy #0
beq in
loop:
jsr $ffd2
iny
in:
lda hello,y
bne loop
rts
hello:  .tx "Hello World!"
        .by 13,10,0
```

68000 Amiga Assembler

; Hello World in 68000 Assembler for dos.library (Amiga)

```
        move.l    #DOS
        move.l    4.w,a6
        jsr       -$0198(a6)        ;OldOpenLibrary
        move.l    d0,a6
        beq.s     .Out
        move.l    #HelloWorld,d1

A)      moveq     #13,d2
        Jsr       -$03AE(a6)        ;WriteChars

B)      jsr       -$03B4           ;PutStr

        move.l    a6,a1
        move.l    4.w,a6
        jsr       -$019E(a6)        ;CloseLibrary
.Out    rts

DOS             dc.b 'dos.library',0
HelloWorld dc.b 'Hello World!',$A,0
```

68000 AtariST Assembler

```
; Hello World in 68000 Assembler (Atari ST)

        move.l   #helloworld,-(A7)
        move     #9,-(A7)
        trap     #1
        addq.l   #6,A7
        move     #0,-(A7)
        trap     #1
helloworld:
        dc.b "Hello World!",$0d,$0a,0
```

8086 Assembler

```
start:
        MOV   AH,09h
        LEA   DX,[msg]
        INT   21h
        MOV   AX,4C00h
        INT   21h
msg:    DB    'Hello, World!$'
```

ABAP

ABAP is an object-oriented programming language created by SAP AG and is used in their SAP Application Server. ABAP's syntax is quite similar to COBOL.

```
* ABAP: "Hello, world!" *
REPORT HELLO_WORLD.
WRITE 'Hello, World!'.
```

ActionScript

ActionScript is an object-oriented language used mainly for the development of websites using the Adobe Flash Player platform. It is an open-source language.

```
trace("Hello, World!");
```

Ada

Ada is a multi-paradigm language that was developed by the United States Department of Defense to replace the numerous languages that were used in the Department. Ada is named after Ada Lovelace.

```
-- Ada: "Hello, World!"
with Ada.Text_IO; use Ada.Text_IO;
procedure Hello is
begin
  Put_Line ("Hello, World!");
end Hello;
```

ALGOL

ALGOrithmic Language (ALGOL) is an imperative language, which was developed in the 1950s, as a language for scientific use.

```
BEGIN
  DISPLAY ("Hello, World!");
END.
```

APL

APL is an array-oriented language that uses symbols rather than words in its syntax, as can be seen in the example below.

```
□←'Hello, World!'
```

AppleScript

AppleScript is a scripting language developed by Apple Inc, which is included in the Macintosh operating systems. It is designed to exchange data between applications and allow control of applications for automating tasks.

```
-- AppleScript: "Hello, world!"
display dialog "Hello, world!"
```

ASP

Active Server Pages (ASP) is a server-side scripting engine for dynamic web pages. ASP pages are normally written using VBScript, as in the example below.

```
<% @ Language="VBScript" %>
<% 'ASP: "Hello, world!"
  Response.Write("<html><body>Hello, world!</body></html>") %>
```

awk

Awk is a programming language that is used for data extraction and reporting and is a standard feature of most Unix operating systems.

```
# awk: "Hello, world!"
BEGIN { print "Hello, world!" }
```

B

B is an extinct programming language that was a forerunner to the popular C language.

```
/* Hello World in B */

main() {
  extern a, b, c;
  putchar (a); putchar (b); putchar (c); putchar ('!*n');
}

a 'hell' ;
b 'o, w' ;
c 'orld' ;
```

BABEL

BABEL is an experimental programming language designed to integrate functional and logical programming.

```
main: { "Goodbye, World!" << }
```

Bash

Bash is a Unix shell designed as a replacement for the Bourne Shell.

```
# Bash: "Hello, world!"
echo Hello, world!
```

BASIC

Beginner's All-purpose Symbolic Instruction Code (BASIC) is a general purpose language which was designed with ease of use in mind. There have been a number of versions of BASIC since it was introduce, with minor differences. The code below is based on the original Dartmouth BASIC.

```
10 REM "Hello World"
20 PRINT "Hello, World!"
30 END
```

BCPL

Basic Combined Programming Language (BCPL) is an imperative programming language that was intended for use in writing compilers for other languages.

```
// Hello world in BCLP
GET "libhdr"

LET start() = VALOF
$( writes("Hello world*N")
      RESULTIS 0
$)
```

Befunge

Befunge is an esoteric programming language that was devised as an attempt to produce a language which was hard to compile as possible.

```
>25*"!dlrow ,olleH":v
                v:,_@
                >  ^
```

Brainf!ck

Brainf!ck is an esoteric programming language that was designed to be as small as possible. The language consists of eight commands, each consisting of a single character.

```
++++++++++[>+++++++>++++++++++>+++<<<-]>++.>+.+++++++
..+++.>++.<<+++++++++++++++.>.+++.------.--------.>+.
```

C

C is a general purpose imperative programming language that is one of the most widely used programming languages of all time.

```
#include <stdlib.h>
#include <stdio.h>

int main(void)
{
  printf("Hello, World!\n");
  return EXIT_SUCCESS;
}
```

C#

C Sharp (C#) is a multi-paradigm language that was developed by Microsoft. It is intended for use as a general-purpose language.

```
System.Console.WriteLine("Hello, World!");
```

C++

C++ is a multi-paradigm general-purpose programming language that initially began as an enhancement to C, adding object-oriented features such as classes.

```
#include <iostream>

int main () {
  std::cout << "Hello, World!" << std::endl;
  return std::cout.bad();
}
```

Chef

Chef is an esoteric programming language that is designed to look like a recipe, with the variables named after ingredients. In the example below potatoes is assigned the value 33, which is the ASCII for 'd'. The method puts all the values for the output into the stack (mixing bowl) and then moves the stack to output (baking dish)

Hello World Souffle.

This recipe prints the immortal words "Hello world!", in a basically brute force
way. It also makes a lot of food for one person.

Ingredients.
72 g haricot beans
101 eggs
108 g lard
111 cups oil
32 zucchinis
119 ml water
114 g red salmon
100 g dijon mustard
33 potatoes

Method.
Put potatoes into the mixing bowl.
Put dijon mustard into the mixing bowl.
Put lard into the mixing bowl.
Put red salmon into the mixing bowl.
Put oil into the mixing bowl.
Put water into the mixing bowl.
Put zucchinis into the mixing bowl.
Put oil into the mixing bowl.
Put lard into the mixing bowl.
Put lard into the mixing bowl.
Put eggs into the mixing bowl.
Put haricot beans into the mixing bowl.
Liquefy contents of the mixing bowl.
Pour contents of the mixing bowl into the baking dish.

Serves 1.

Clean

Clean is a general-purpose functional programming language influenced by Haskell.

```
module hello
Start :: {#Char}
Start = "Hello, world!"
```

COBOL

Common Business-Oriented Language (COBOL) is one of the original high-level programming languages, designed for use in business rather than scientific environments.

```
program-id. hello.
procedure division.
      display "Hello, World!".
      stop run.
```

ColdFusion Markup Language

ColdFusion MArkup Language is a scripting language used for web development.

```
<cfoutput>Hello, World!</cfoutput>
```

Component Pascal

Component Pascal is a multi-paradigm programming language. Despite bearing the name of Pascal, it is incompatible with it.

```
MODULE Hello;
  IMPORT Out;

  PROCEDURE Do*;
  BEGIN
      Out.String("Hello, World!"); Out.Ln
  END Do;
END Hello.
```

COOL

Classroom Object-Oriented Language (COOL) is an object-oriented programming language designed for use in an undergraduate course project.

```
-- Hello World in Cool

class Main inherits IO{
  main():Object{
  out_string("Hello, world!\n")
  };
};
```

CYBOL

Cybernetics Oriented Language (CYBOL) is a knowledge modelling and programming language that is based on XML.

```
<!-- Hello World in Cybernetics Oriented Language (CYBOL) -->
<model>
    <part name="send_message" channel="inline"
abstraction="operation" model="send">
        <property name="channel" channel="inline"
abstraction="character" model="shell"/>
        <property name="message" channel="inline"
abstraction="character" model="Hello, World!"/>
    </part>
    <part name="exit_application" channel="inline"
abstraction="operation" model="exit"/>
</model>
```

D

D is a multi-paradigm programming language that is influenced by C++, Java, Python and a number of other languages.

```
// Hello World in D

import std.stdio;

void main()
{
  writefln("Hello World!");
}
```

Dart

Dart is an object-oriented web programming language designed by Google. It is an open source language and its intention is to replace JavaScript as the main language of web development.

```
main() {
  var bye = Hello, World!';
  print("$bye");
}
```

dBase

The dBase programming language is the internal language of the dBase database system. It is primarily used for opening, traversing and manipulating records in the database.

```
* dBase IV: "Hello, world!"
? "Hello, world!"
```

Delphi

Delphi is a dialect of Pascal and is written using the Embarcadero Delphi integrated development environment.

```
program ProjectHello;
{$APPTYPE CONSOLE}
begin
  WriteLn(Hello, World!');
end.
```

Dylan

Dylan is a multi-paradigm programming language that is derived from Scheme and Common Lisp.

```
// Hello World in DYLAN

define method main (#rest args)
  princ("Hello world!");
end;

main();
```

Eiffel

Eiffel is an object-oriented programming language. The language included a number of concepts that would later be integrated into other languages such as Java and C♯.

```
indexing
  description: "Eiffel: Hello, world!"
class
  HELLO_WORLD
create
  make
feature
  make
      do
            print ("Hello, World!%N")
      end
end
```

Erlang

Erlang is a multi-paradigm programming language that was developed by Ericsson to support distributed non-stop applications.

```
%% Hello World in Erlang

-module(hello).

-export([hello/0]).

hello() ->
    io:format("Hello World!~n", []).
```

Fjölnir

Fjölnir is an Icelandic programming language, which is based on the concept of representing programs as trees.

```
;; Hello World in Fjölnir (Icelandic programming language)

"hello" < main
{
  main ->
  stef(;)
  stofn
       skrifastreng(;"Halló Veröld!"),
  stofnlok
}
*
"GRUNNUR"
;
```

Forth

Forth is an imperative programming language. There are a number of dialects of the Forth language. The code below is written in Gforth which is an implementation by the GNU project.

```
\ Gforth: "Hello, world!"
s" world!" s" Hello, "
type type CR
bye
```

Fortran

FORmula TRANslating System (FORTRAN) is another of the early high-level languages, which was designed for scientific and engineering applications.

```
C     Fortran: Hello, world!
      PROGRAM HALLO
      WRITE (*,100)
      STOP
  100 FORMAT ('Hello, world!')
      END
```

G

G is a graphical dataflow programming language used in the LabVIEW development environment. There is no source code, everything is programmed graphically.

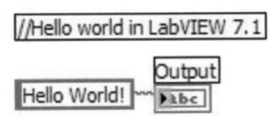

Go

Go is an imperative programming language that is being developed by Google. Go's syntax is broadly similar to that of C.

```
package main

func main() { println("Hello, World!") }
```

Gofer

GOod For Equational Reasoning (Gofer) is an implementation of Haskell that is intended for educational purposes.

```
-- Hello World in Gofer
-- Dialog version

helloWorld :: Dialogue
helloWorld resps = [AppendChan stdout "Hello world!"]
```

Groovy

Groovy is an object-oriented scripting language that is designed to run on the Java Virtual Machine platform.

```
// Groovy: "Hello, world!"
println "Hello, world!"
```

Haskell

Haskell is a general-purpose functional programming language. It is named after the logician Haskell Curry.

```
-- Haskell: "Hello, world!"
main :: IO ()
main = putStrLn "Hello, world!"
```

Hello

Hello is a joke esoteric programming language that has only one instruction (h). The instruction prints "Hello World", giving, along with the HQ9+ language mentioned later, the most compact implementation of the Hello World program.

```
h
```

HQ9+

HQ9+ is a joke esoteric programming language, which has only 4 instructions (H, Q,) and +). One instruction 'H' prints "Hello, World!", giving, along with the Hello language mentioned earlier, the most compact implementation of the Hello World program.

```
H
```

HTML

HyperText Markup Language (HTML) is a markup language that is used for displaying web pages.

```
<!DOCTYPE HTML PUBLIC "-//W3C//DTD HTML 4.01//EN">
<!-- HTML: "Hello, world!" -->
<html>
  <head>
      <title>Hello World</title>
      <meta http-equiv="Content-Type" content="text/html;
  charset=UTF-8">
  </head>
  <body>
      <p>Hello, World!</p>
  </body>
</html>
```

HyperTalk

HyperTalk is a procedural programming language used with Apple Computer's HyperCard hypermedia program.

```
-- Hello World in HyperTalk

answer "Hello, world!"
```

Inform 6

Inform 6 is a object-oriented programming language designed for writing interactive fiction.

```
[ Main;
  print "Hello World^";
];
```

INTERCAL

Intercal is an esoteric programming language created to satirise various languages available when it was developed.

```
* INTERCAL: "Hello, world!" INTERCAL
PLEASE DO ,1 <- #13
DO ,1 SUB #1 <- #238
DO ,1 SUB #2 <- #112
DO ,1 SUB #3 <- #112
DO ,1 SUB #4 <- #0
DO ,1 SUB #5 <- #64
DO ,1 SUB #6 <- #238
DO ,1 SUB #7 <- #26
DO ,1 SUB #8 <- #248
DO ,1 SUB #9 <- #168
DO ,1 SUB #10 <- #24
DO ,1 SUB #11 <- #16
DO ,1 SUB #12 <- #158
DO ,1 SUB #13 <- #52
DO READ OUT ,1
PLEASE GIVE UP
```

Io

Io is a pure object-oriented programming language that was inspired by Smalltalk.

```
// Hello World in io programming language
"Hello world!" println
```

J

J is a functional programming language that is based on APL, FP and FL languages. J is most often used in mathematical and statistical programming

```
NB. Hello World in J
'Hello World' 1!:2(2)
```

Java

Java is an object-oriented language that was designed to be as platform independent as possible. Java applications are normally compiled into bytecode that is run on a Java Virtual Machine.

```
// Java: "Hello, world!"
class HelloWorld {
  public static void main(String args[]) {
      System.out.println("Hello, world!");
  }
}
```

Java (Swing)

Swing is the main Java GUI widget toolkit, which was developed to provide a sophisticated set of GUI components.

```
// Hello World in Java using Swing GUI

class HelloWorldSwing {
  static public void main(String args[]) {
      javax.swing.JOptionPane.showMessageDialog(null,"Hello
world!");
  }
}
```

JavaScript

JavaScript is a client-side scripting language that is used in web browsers to create dynamic websites. The code example below is designed to be embedded in an HTML document and will output the text string to the browser.

```
<script type="text/javascript">
  document.write('Hello, world!');
</script>
```

JCL

Job Control Language (JCL) is a scripting language used on IBM mainframe operating systems to instruct the system how to run a batch job.

```
//HERIB   JOB ,'HERIBERT OTTEN',PRTY=12
//* HELLO WORLD FOR MVS
  //HALLO      EXEC PGM=IEBGENER
  //SYSIN      DD DUMMY
  //SYSPRINT   DD SYSOUT=*
  //SYSUT2     DD SYSOUT=T
  //SYSUT1     DD *
  HELLO WORLD!
  /*
  //
```

K

K is an array processing language that serves as the foundation for kdb, an in-memory column-based database.

```
/ Hello World in K

`0:"Hello World!\n
```

KiXtart

KiXtart is a scripting language for Windows that provides automation for Windows programs. In the example below, the code opens Notepad and types the phrase "Hello, World!"

```
; Hello World in Kix

Run( "Notepad.exe" )
Sleep 1
SetFocus( "Untitled - Notepad" )
$ReturnCode = SendKeys("Hello World")
Sleep( 2 )
$ReturnCode = SendKeys("~{F4}Y")
```

L

L is an object-oriented programming language with a C-like syntax.

```
namespace HelloWorld is
  class Main is
      // Program execution starts at Main.init():
      void init() is
          // IO.Std.out refers the program's standard output:
          IO.Std.out.println( "Hello World!" );
      si
  si
si
```

LaTeX

LATEX is a document markup language for the TeX typesetting program.

```
% LaTeX: "Hello, world!"
\documentclass{article}
\begin{document}
Hello, world!
\end{document}
```

Limbo

Limbo is a programming language for writing distributed systems. The Limbo compiler produces object code that can be interpreted by a virtual machine.

```
implement Command;

include "sys.m";
  sys: Sys;

include "draw.m";

include "sh.m";

init(nil: ref Draw->Context, nil: list of string)
{
  sys = load Sys Sys->PATH;
  sys->print("Hello World!\n");
}
```

Lisaac

Lisaac is an object-oriented programming language. The language is influenced by Smalltalk, Self and Eiffel.

```
Section Header
  + name := GOODBYE;

Section Public
  - main <- ("Goodbye, World!\n".print;);
```

Linotte

Linotte is a fourth generation programming language that is unique in that its syntax is in French.

```
Livre : Hello
  Paragraphe : display message
  Actions :
      Affiche "Hello World!"
      Termine
```

Lisp

Lisp is the second oldest high-level programming language, having been specified in 1958. There are a number of List dialects and the code below is written in Common Lisp.

```
(format t "Hello, World!~%")
```

Logo

Logo is a multi-paradigm programming language that was designed for use in education. It is an adaptation of Lisp.

```
print [Hello, World!]
```

Machine Code

Machine code is the lowest level programming language possible. Each instruction in a machine code program performs one specific task such as storing a value in a register.

Machine code is normally written in binary format, but for brevity I have converted it to hexadecimal here. If it were written in 8-bit binary, the first two commands (B4 and 09) would look like this –

```
10110100 00001001
```

```
B4 09 8D 16 0D 01 CD 21  B8 00 4C CD 21 48 65 6C 6C 6F 2C 20
77 6F 72 6C 64 21 24
```

MACRO-10

MACRO-10 is an assembly language that has extensive macro facilities. It is used on DEC's PDP-10 minicomputer systems.

```
        TITLE  HELLO WORLD
        ; 'Hello world' in MACRO-10 for TOPS-10
        SEARCH     UUOSYM

LAB:    ASCIZ    /Hello, world!

START:  RESET
OUTPUT: OUTSTR    LAB
        MONRT
        JRST      OUTPUT
        END    START
```

MACRO-11

MACRO-11 is an assembly language that has macro facilities. It is used on DEC's PDP-11 minicomputer systems.

```
;               "Hello, world!" in MACRO-11 for RT-11

        .MCALL      .EXIT,.PRINT
START:  .PRINT      #$1
        .EXIT
$1:     .ASCIZ      /Hello, world!/
        .END        START
```

Malbolge

Malbolge is an esoteric programming language that was specifically designed to be impossible to write useful programs in.

```
('&%:9]!~}|z2Vxwv-,POqponl$Hjig%eB@@>}=<M:9wv6WsU2T|nm-
,jcL(I&%$#"
 `CB]V?Tx<uVtT`Rpo3NlF.Jh++FdbCBA@?]!~|4XzyTT43Qsqq(Lnmkj"
Fhg${z@>
```

Mathematica

Mathematica is a software program used for scientific, engineering and mathematical projects. It includes the Mathematica language as part of the package.

```
Print["Hello, World!"]
```

MATLAB

MATLAB is a multi-paradigm fourth-generation programming language.

```
>> Hello, World!'

ans =

Hello, World!
```

Mercury

Mercury is a functional logic programming language influenced by Prolog and Haskell.

```
:- module hello.
:- interface.
:- import_module io.
:- pred main(io::di, io::uo) is det.

:- implementation.
main(!IO) :-
  io.write_string("Hello, World!\n", !IO).
```

Modula-2

Modula-2 is an imperative programming language developed as a revision of Pascal.

```
(* Modula-2: "Hello, world!" *)
MODULE Hello;
IMPORT InOut;

BEGIN
  InOut.WriteString('Hello, World!');
  InOut.WriteLn
END Hello.
```

Modula-3

Modula-3 is an imperative programming language that was conceived as a follow on to Modula-2.

```
(* Hello World in Modula-3 *)

MODULE Hello EXPORTS Main;

IMPORT IO;

BEGIN
  IO.Put("Hello World!\n");
END Hello.
```

MOO

MOO is the programming language used in the MOO text-based online virtual reality game system.

```
player.location:announce_all("Hello, world!");
```

MUMPS

MUMPS is a procedural programming language designed for use in the healthcare industry.

```
; Hello World in Mumps-M
  w !,"Hello World"
```

NewtonScript

NewtonScript is an object-oriented programming language developed by Apple' Newton PDA Platrorm.

```
// Hello World in NewtonScript

baseview :=
  {viewBounds: {left: -3, top: 71, right: 138, bottom: 137},
   viewFlags: 581,
   declareSelf: 'base,
   _proto: protoFloatNGo,
   debug: "baseview"
  };

textview := * child of baseview *
  {text: "Hello World!",
   viewBounds: {left: 33, top: 24, right: 113, bottom: 46},
   viewFlags: 579,
   _proto: protoStaticText,
   debug: "textview"
  };
```

NXC

Not eXactly C (NXC) is a programming language for the Lego Mindstorms NXT programmable robotics kit. It has a C-like syntax.

```
/* Hello World in NXC ("Not Exactly C") */

#include "NXCDefs.h"

task main()
{
  TextOut(0, LCD_LINE1, "Hello World!");
}
```

Oberon

Oberon is an imperative programming language, developed as part of the Oberon operating system.

```
(* Oberon: "Hello, world!" *)
MODULE Helloworld;
IMPORT Write;
BEGIN
  Write.Line("Hello, world!");
END Helloworld.
```

occam

occam is an imperative programming language based on Communicating Sequential Processes process algebra.

```
PROGRAM Hello
-- Hello world in Occam
#USE ioconv

SEQ
  write.full.string(screen,"Hello World!")
```

Ook!

Ook! is a joke esoteric programming language that is identical to Brainf!ck, just with the commands changed to 'orang-utan language'.

```
Ook. Ook? Ook. Ook. Ook. Ook. Ook. Ook. Ook. Ook. Ook. Ook.
Ook. Ook. Ook. Ook. Ook. Ook. Ook. Ook. Ook! Ook? Ook? Ook.
Ook. Ook. Ook. Ook. Ook. Ook. Ook. Ook. Ook. Ook. Ook. Ook.
Ook. Ook. Ook. Ook. Ook? Ook! Ook! Ook? Ook! Ook? Ook. Ook!
Ook. Ook. Ook? Ook. Ook. Ook. Ook. Ook. Ook. Ook. Ook. Ook.
Ook. Ook. Ook.Ook. Ook. Ook! Ook? Ook? Ook. Ook. Ook. Ook.
Ook. Ook. Ook. Ook. Ook. Ook. Ook? Ook! Ook! Ook? Ook! Ook?
Ook. Ook. Ook. Ook! Ook. Ook. Ook. Ook. Ook. Ook. Ook. Ook.
Ook. Ook. Ook. Ook. Ook. Ook. Ook! Ook. Ook! Ook. Ook. Ook.
Ook. Ook. Ook. Ook! Ook. Ook. Ook? Ook. Ook? Ook. Ook? Ook.
Ook. Ook. Ook. Ook. Ook. Ook. Ook. Ook. Ook. Ook. Ook. Ook.
Ook. Ook. Ook! Ook? Ook? Ook. Ook. Ook. Ook. Ook. Ook. Ook.
Ook. Ook. Ook. Ook? Ook! Ook! Ook? Ook! Ook? Ook. Ook! Ook.
Ook. Ook? Ook. Ook? Ook. Ook? Ook. Ook. Ook. Ook. Ook. Ook.
Ook. Ook. Ook. Ook. Ook. Ook. Ook. Ook. Ook. Ook. Ook. Ook.
Ook. Ook! Ook? Ook? Ook. Ook. Ook. Ook. Ook. Ook. Ook. Ook.
Ook. Ook. Ook. Ook. Ook. Ook. Ook. Ook. Ook. Ook. Ook. Ook.
Ook? Ook! Ook! Ook? Ook! Ook? Ook. Ook! Ook! Ook! Ook! Ook!
Ook! Ook! Ook. Ook? Ook. Ook? Ook. Ook? Ook. Ook? Ook. Ook!
Ook. Ook. Ook. Ook. Ook. Ook. Ook. Ook! Ook. Ook! Ook! Ook! Ook!
Ook! Ook! Ook! Ook! Ook! Ook! Ook! Ook! Ook! Ook. Ook! Ook! Ook!
Ook! Ook! Ook! Ook! Ook! Ook! Ook! Ook! Ook! Ook! Ook! Ook! Ook!
Ook! Ook. Ook. Ook? Ook. Ook? Ook. Ook. Ook! Ook. Ook! Ook?
Ook! Ook! Ook? Ook! Ook. Ook. Ook. Ook. Ook. Ook. Ook. Ook.
Ook. Ook. Ook. Ook. Ook. Ook. Ook. Ook. Ook. Ook. Ook. Ook!
Ook.
```

Oxygene

Oxygene is an object-oriented programming language that is based on Object Pascal.

```
namespace HelloWorld;

interface

type
  HelloClass = class
  public
      class method Main;
  end;

implementation

class method HelloClass.Main;
begin
  System.Console.WriteLine(Hello, World!');
end;

end.
```

Oz

Oz is a multi-paradigm programming language that is influenced by Erlang, Lisp and Prolog

```
% Hello World in Oz

functor
import
  System
  Application
define
  {System.showInfo "Hello World!"}
  {Application.exit 0}
end
```

Pascal

Pascal is an imperative programming language named after the French mathematician Blaise Pascal.

```
program helloworld;
(* Pascal: Hello, world! *)
begin
  writeln(Hello, World!');
end.
```

Perl

Perl is a multi-paradigm programming language. It was initially developed as a general-purpose Unix scripting language for report processing.

```
# Perl: "Hello, world!"
print "Hello, World!\n";
```

PHP

PHP is a server-side scripting language used for producing dynamic web pages. It is an open-source language and can be embedded directly into an HTML document.

```
<?php
  // PHP: "Hello, world!"
  echo "<html><body>"."Hello, world!"."</body></html>";
?>
```

Piet

Piet is an esoteric programming language whose programs are bitmaps that resemble abstract art. Commands are defined by the transition of colour from one colour block to the next. The number of steps along the Hue Cycle and Lightness Cycle in each transition determine the command executed.

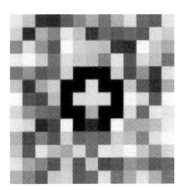

PL/1

PL/1 (Programming Language One) is an imperative programming language developed by IBM. It was designed as a single programming language for business and scientific users.

```
/* PL/1: "Hello, world!" */
Hello: procedure options(main);
  put skip list('Hello, world!');
end Hello;
```

PL/SQL

PL/SQL is a procedural extension language for SQL for use in Oracle's relational databases.

```
SET SERVEROUTPUT ON;
BEGIN
  DBMS_OUTPUT.PUT_LINE('Hello, world!');
END;
```

Plankalkül

Plankalkül was the first high-level programming language to be designed. Although it was designed over a decade before FORTRAN, it was not implemented at the time.

```
R1.1(V0[:sig]) => R0
R1.2(V0[:m x sig]) => R0
0 => i | m + 1 => j
[W [ i < j -> [ R1.1(V0[i: m x sig]) => R0 | i + 1 => i ] ] ]
END
R1.3() => R0
'H';'e';'l';'l';'o';',';' ';'w';'o';'r';'l';'d';'!' => Z0[: m x sig]
R1.2(Z0) => R0
END
```

PostScript

PostScript is a multi-paradigm programming language developed by Adobe Systems. It is often used as a page description language for desktop publishing.

```
% Hello World in Postscript
%!PS
/Palatino-Roman findfont
100 scalefont
setfont
100 100 moveto
(Hello World!) show
Showpage
```

Prolog

Prolog is a general purpose logical programming language often used in artificial intelligence.

```
% Prolog: "Hello, world!"
?- write('Hello, world!') , nl .
```

Python

Python is a multi-paradigm general purpose programming language that has been designed with code readability in mind.

```
# Python: "Hello, world!"
print "Hello, world!"
```

Qore

Qore is a multi-paradigm general-purpose programming language with a syntax similar to Perl.

```
#!/usr/local/bin/qore
# Hello World in qore

class HelloWorld
{
  constructor()
  {
      background $.output("Hello, world!");
  }
  output($arg)
  {
      printf("%s\n", $arg);
  }
}

new HelloWorld();
```

Refal

Recursive functions algorithmic language (Refal) is a functional programming language that is based on pattern matching.

```
$ENTRY Go { = <Hello>;}
Hello {
  = <Prout 'Hello world'>;
}
```

RPG

RPG is a multi-paradigm programming language developed by IBM in 1959 The current version is RPG IV.

```
H* Hello World in RPG IV

D msg          S          32   inz(*blank)
D cmd          S          64

C              eval       msg = 'Hello World'

C      msg     dsply

C              eval       cmd = 'DLYJOB DLY(30)'
C              call       'QCMDEXC'
C              parm                cmd
C              parm       64       len           15 5

C              eval       *inlr = *on
```

RTL/2

RTL/2 was an imperative programming language designed for use in real-time computing.

```
TITLE Hello World;

LET NL=10;

EXT PROC(REF ARRAY BYTE) TWRT;

ENT PROC RRJOB() INT;

  TWRT("Hello, World!#NL#");
  RETURN(1);

ENDPROC;
```

Ruby

Ruby is a multi-paradigm programming language that has a Perl inspired syntax together with Smalltalk-like features.

```
# Ruby: "Hello, world!"
puts "Hello, world!"
```

SAS

The SAS language is a statistical analysis and data processing language used in the SAS (Statistical Analysis System) software package.

```
/* Hello world in SAS */
* Writes as output title;
TITLE "Hello World!";
* writes to the log;
PUT Hello world!;
```

Sather

Sather is an object-oriented programming language that was originally based on Eiffel.

```
class HELLO_WORLD is
  main is
      #OUT+"Hello World\n";
  end;
end;
```

Scala

Scala is a multi-paradigm programming language designed to be an improvement on Java. It runs on the Java Virtual Machine, so is platform independent.

```
// Hello World in Scala

object HelloWorld with Application {
  Console.println("Hello world!");
}
```

Scheme

Scheme is a multi-paradigm programming language and is a dialect of Lisp.

```
;;; Scheme: "Hello, world!"
(define h(lambda()(display "\nHello, world!")(newline)()))(h)
```

sed

sed is a Unix utility that is used for text parsing and transformation. It is a primitive language, but can perform powerful data processing from within shell scripts.

```
echo s | sed -ne '1s/.*/Hello, world!/p'
```

Seed7

Seed7 is a multi-paradigm general-purpose programming language that is syntactically similar to Pascal and Ada.

```
$ include "seed7_05.s7i";

const proc: main is func
  begin
      writeln("Hello, World!");
  end func;
```

Self

Self is an object-oriented programming language and is a dialect of Smalltalk.

```
'Hello, world!' print.
```

Shell (Bourne Shell)

Bourne Shell is a command-line interface for the Unix operating system. Whilst mainly used as a command interpreter, it has all the features of a scripting language.

```
echo Hello, world!
```

Simula

Simula is an object-oriented programming language based on ALGOL 60. It is considered the first object-oriented language.

```
Begin
  OutText ("Hello World!");
  Outimage;
End;
```

SISAL

SISAL is a general-purpose functional programming language with a Pascal-like syntax.

```
define main

type string = array[character];

function main(returns string)
  "Goodbye, World!"
end function
```

Smalltalk (simple version)

Smalltalk is a pure object-oriented programming language, which means that all data types are stored as objects.

This code example assumes that a Transcript window is open.

```
"Hello World in Smalltalk (simple version)"

Transcript show: 'Hello, World!'.
```

Smalltalk (window version)

This second Smalltalk example will open its own window to display the output.

```
"Hello World in Smalltalk (in an own window)"
"(to be entered in a special browser)"

VisualComponent subclass: #HelloWorldView
  instanceVariableNames: ''
  classVariableNames: ''
  poolDictionaries: ''
  category: 'test'

displayOn: aGraphicsContext

  'Hello World!' asComposedText displayOn: aGraphicsContext.

open

  |window|
  window := ScheduledWindow new.
  window label: 'Hello World Demo:'.
  window component: self new.
  window open.
```

SQL

Structured Query Language (SQL) is a special-purpose programming language for working with data in a relational database.

There are various flavours of SQL from the different database vendors. Below are a few examples.

```
SELECT 'Hello, World!' FROM DUAL; -- Oracle version.
SELECT 'Hello, World!' FROM SYSIBM.SysDummy1-- DB2 version
SELECT 'Hello, World!' -- SQL Server version.
```

Thue

Thue is an esoteric programming language based on semi-Thue grammar.

```
a::=~Hello, World!
::=
a
```

Unlambda

Unlambda is a functional programming language that is based on combinatory logic. The language has no variables.

```
`r```````````.H.e.l.l.o.,. .w.o.r.l.d.!i
```

Vala

Vala is an object-oriented programming language that has a similar syntax to C♯.

```
class Sample : Object {
  void greeting() {
      stdout.printf("Hello World\n");
  }

  static void main(string[] args) {
      var sample = new Sample();
      sample.greeting();
  }
}
```

Vatical

Vatical is an esoteric programming language with a religious flavour.

```
+ Hello World in Vatical

LITURGY:
  PRAY "Hello World!"
AMEN.
```

VAX Macro

VAX Macro is the assembly language implementation for CPUs running DEC's OpenVMS operating system.

```
        .title  helloworld
        .ident  /hello world/
;
        .library        /sys$library:lib/
        $libdef
        $lib$routinesdef

        .psect  $data,wrt,noshr,noexe,long

hello:  .ascid  /Hello, World!/

        .psect  $code,nowrt,shr,exe,long

        .entry  helloworld,^m<r9,r10,r11>

        Pushaq  hello
        Calls   #1,g^lib$put_output

        ret
        .end    helloworld
```

VBScript

VBScript is a scripting language developed by Microsoft that is based on Visual Basic.

```
' Hello World in VBScript (Windows Scripting Host)
msgbox "Hello, World!"
```

Visual Basic

Visual Basic is a derivative of BASIC developed by Microsoft. It is designed to be an event-driven language with modules run when events such as clicking on a button in the GUI occur. A cut down version of the language Visual Basic for Applications (VBA) is supplied with the Microsoft Office package.

```
REM Hello World in Visual Basic for Windows

VERSION 2.00
Begin Form Form1
  Caption        =    "Form1"
  ClientHeight   =    6096
  ClientLeft=    936
  ClientTop=    1572
  ClientWidth    =    6468
  Height         =    6540
  Left           =    876
  LinkTopic=    "Form1"
  ScaleHeight    =    6096
  ScaleWidth     =    6468
  Top            =    1188
  Width          =    6588
  Begin Label Label1
        Caption    =    "Hello, World!"
        Height     =    372
        Left       =    2760
        TabIndex=    0
        Top        =    2880
        Width      =    972
  End
End
Option Explicit
```

Visual Basic .Net

Visual Basic .Net is an object-oriented language that forms part of Microsoft's .Net Framework. It is often seen as an evolution of Visual Basic, with the versioning starting from V7.0 (the last Visual Basic was VB6).

```
Class Form1
  Public Sub Form1_Load(ByVal sender As Object, ByVal e As
  EventArgs) Handles Me.Load()
      MsgBox("Hello, world!")
  End Sub
End Class
```

XML

Extensible Markup Language (XML) is a markup language that defines rules for encoding documents in a format that is readable by both machines and humans. XML document formats are used by recent versions of Microsoft Office as well as Open Office.

```
<?xml version="1.0" encoding="ISO-8859-1"?>
<?xml-stylesheet type="text/xsl" href="HelloWorld.xsl" ?>
<!-- Hello World in XML -->
<greet>
  <how>Hello,</how>
  <who>world</who>
  <mark>!</mark>
</greet>
```

XPL0

XPL0 is a programming language that is a cross between Pascal and C.

```
code Text=12;
  Text(0, "Hello, World!")
```

ABOUT THE AUTHOR

Professor James Steinberg is a Professor of Applied Computing, lecturing on programming in a number of current and historical programming languages.

Professor Steinberg also acts in a consultancy role for a number of software development companies, advising on the implementation of corporate systems.

Professor Steinberg is an avid proponent of the Open Source movement and regularly lectures on the benefits of the Open Source paradigm.

Professor Steinberg is married with two children.

More information about Professor Steinberg and the other books he has written can be found at http://www.jamessteinberg.info.

OTHER BOOKS BY THE AUTHOR

Open Office Basic: An Introduction

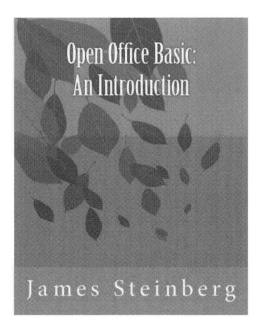

Apache Open Office is the leading open-source office software suite. It features word processing, spreadsheets, presentations, graphics and databases. It is available for all major operating systems. Open Office has the ability to automate features using recorded and manually created macros, created using a number of different programming languages. This book concentrates on one of those languages OpenOffice.org Basic. This book starts by giving an overview of the language and its structure, before detailing the various commands and functions that are available in OpenOffice.org Basic.

Open Office Basic: An Introduction is available in Paperback (ISBN 1481270931) and as a Kindle eBook from your local Amazon website.

Made in the USA
Middletown, DE
11 October 2020

21706683R00073